"In an era of fracture and fear, withdrawal may seem easier than engagement. Lowell Greathouse challenges this instinct. With a reminder that we only endure together, he offers a treasury of simple (and challenging!) practices that compassionately call us back to ourselves, to one another, and to action. More than a book for just this moment, it is a guide for each unsettled season."

—**Karyn Richards-Kuan**
Senior Pastor, First United Methodist Church of Portland

"*Navigating Trumpworld* maps paths of healing and renewal to help American democracy survive the Trump 2.0 turbulence that endangers it. Lowell Greathouse's 'rallying cry directed at hearts' resounds persuasively with wisdom, insight, and urgency. If we Americans follow where he leads, our country, ourselves, will get back on track."

—**John K. Roth**
Edward J. Sexton Professor Emeritus of Philosophy, Claremont McKenna College

"Curiosity, attentiveness, gratefulness—what affect do such practices have in our context of political and social upheavals? Greathouse clearly names the hostility and destructiveness of Trumpworld. Then he names practices that can connect our inner lives with our social contexts so we can counter tendencies of avoidance, rage, hopelessness, and isolation. Greathouse brings years of pastoring, activism, praying, reading, listening, and collaborating into the challenges we are facing. The practices that he names can bring life and hope into our lives, churches, and society."

—**Mark Lau Branson**
Senior Professor of Practical Theology, Fuller Theological Seminary

"It is a delicate dance not to trip up and stumble through—boldly calling out the evils of violation while embodying a compassion that extends to all. Lowell Greathouse shows us how to dance this dance with grace. Even in the midst of pain and oppression, he hears the music that emboldens the spirit; and he offers dance steps to be taken up into the song's liberative rhythms. If you are seeking a way to keep your soul alive during these crushing times, partner with Greathouse. Let *Navigating Trumpworld* serve as your guide. In the midst of it all, it shows us how to move in time with the restorative divine."

—**Frank Rogers Jr.**
Co-Director, Center for Engaged Compassion

Navigating Trumpworld

Navigating Trumpworld

A Spiritual Guide for Turbulent Times

LOWELL GREATHOUSE

RESOURCE *Publications* • Eugene, Oregon

NAVIGATING TRUMPWORLD
A Spiritual Guide for Turbulent Times

Resource Publications
An Imprint of Wipf and Stock Publishers
199 W. 8th Ave., Suite 3
Eugene, OR 97401

www.wipfandstock.com

PAPERBACK ISBN: 979-8-3852-5648-8
HARDCOVER ISBN: 979-8-3852-5649-5
EBOOK ISBN: 979-8-3852-5650-1

VERSION NUMBER 082125

To my loving parents and my brothers, Mark and Gordon, who from the very beginning taught me about the spiritual values that matter most in life, and to Susan and my daughters, Lindsey and Kelly, and grandsons, Riley and Declan, who will inherit the world we leave behind.

And

In memory of Devon Hartman.

Contents

Acknowledgments

IT HAS OFTEN BEEN said that it takes a village to raise a child. It is also true that it takes a village to be a village. Everyone's presence matters in every human situation.

I have been the beneficiary of a number of real and metaphorical villages in my life, including my family of origin, the family that Susan and I created with our daughters, the various schools I have attended, and the workplaces and communities I have been a part of over the years. Each of these villages has contributed to my spiritual growth and learning. This means that countless people have contributed to making this book possible through the conversations, insights, and challenges that have been a part of each of those settings. The insights I have learned in these places have shaped my spirit and informed how I see the world.

This, of course, has been grounded in the love and journey that Susan and I have shared with each other since 1982. Our relationship has been an anchor in my life, and our lifelong partnership is one of my life's blessings.

But the first "village" I was a part of involved my parents and brothers, Mark and Gordon, who provided a spiritually grounded place to begin life and encouraged me to follow my passions and interests. That setting not only hardwired my spirit but established the software that has become who I am in my personal and public life. This ongoing sense of family has been an important part of my spiritual journey, and I feel a deep sense of gratitude for my family and how that village has shaped me as a person.

I've also been blessed with countless teachers and mentors, who have helped form my understanding of both democracy and spirituality: Jim Barlow, John Whiteneck, Doug Nelson, John Roth, John Snortum, Alpheus Mason, Fred Krensky, Franklin Tugwell, Mary Harris, Paulo Freire, Marvin Chandler, Will Lightbourne, Eileen Purcell, Richard Foster, Parker Palmer, Duane Medicine Crow, Rene Pino, and Frank Rogers, to name but a few. Having thoughtful mentors, colleagues, and teachers in one's life makes a world of difference, and I have been richly blessed beyond measure.

I have also been fortunate to be a part of many learning laboratories over the years, which have helped form my understanding of spiritual life and political realities: the model political conventions that I participated in during middle school and high school in 1968 and 1972 thanks to Jim Barlow; the Claremont Colleges as a diverse educational setting that broadened my understanding of life; the independent studies related to the Social Gospel, Neo-orthodoxy, and liberation theology that I did at Claremont with Dr. Roth; the conversations with Mike Smith, Devon Hartman, and Mark Branson during our time together as housemates at Claremont; Oregon Fair Share; the Graduate Theological Union in the Bay Area; the Cuernavaca Center for Intercultural Dialogue on Development; Catholic Social Services of San Francisco; United Way of the Columbia-Willamette; the congregations where I served as pastor in Filer, Idaho, and in Lake Oswego, Beaverton, and Portland, Oregon; the Greater Northwest Area UMC Cabinet that I was a part of from 2010–2019; numerous cross-cultural settings; the Writers in the Grove; and Oregon Humanities.

Each group has been a part of the village I have been involved with at one time or another, and each of these settings has helped shape my views and ultimately the practices I outline in *Navigating Trumpworld*.

I also want to thank those who read and gave feedback to the early drafts of *Navigating Trumpworld*: Gordon Greathouse, John Roth, Mark and Helena Greathouse, Ann Farley, Kristinoel Ludwig, the Writers in the Grove, and my wife, Susan. Their insights and critique helped shape this book and make it better than it would have been without their encouragement, insightful comments, and contributions.

Finally, many thanks to the gifted staff at Wipf and Stock Publishers. Their professional expertise and guidance have been invaluable. Without their support and assistance, this work would not have seen the light of day.

It takes a village to be a village, and in this case, it takes a village to create a book. Thanks to everyone who has touched my life over the years and helped me grow as a human being. From my experience, I've learned that spirituality is a very precious and personal thing, but it cannot reach fruition or plumb the depths of one's soul without the contributions and challenges that come from living in community with others. A simple thank you seems inadequate, but from thanksgiving comes a sense of gratitude, and I am deeply grateful to so many.

Introduction

How the Hell Did We Get Here Anyway?

A strong community helps people develop a sense of true self, for only in community can the self exercise and fulfill its nature: giving and taking, listening and speaking, being and doing. But when community unravels and we lose touch with one another, the self atrophies and we lose touch with ourselves as well.

—Parker Palmer

As NEIGHBORS SHARING SPACE with each other, we are all part of a giant, elaborate, ongoing dance. This dance engages our true selves and the various competing interests and agendas of the communities we inhabit.

The dance floor covers both political life and our spiritual well-being. When things are going well, we feel free to dance to the music that moves our spirits, and the dance floor is a safe place for everyone.

The music we listen to and enjoy most determines who we feel comfortable with as dance partners and where we end up on the dance floor. It also determines how big this space is and whether or not it is welcoming to everyone or if it is an exclusive club open only to those who appreciate a certain type of music.

Today, there is a variety of music playing in communities throughout the country, from rock and roll to R&B, country to heavy metal, folk, reggae, blues, jazz, Latin, Cajun, and rap, and from classical to soul. Each one brings something special to the table and is competing for our attention and wanting us to dance to their unique beat. The truth is, we can enjoy and appreciate them all.

The music that moves us impacts and ultimately determines both our sense of true self and the type of communities we create and live in. While we each have our own personal preferences, the common thread is that every genre represents some form of music. Collectively, they portray an amazing kaleidoscope of human creativity, diversity, and expression.

In the current version of our national dance, there are distinct types of music that fill the air. And when you listen closely, you realize that there is an important difference between monologues and conversations. Between uniformity and diversity. Between a closed fist and an open hand. Between condemnation and forgiveness. Between fear and love. Between division and community. There is a fundamental difference between authoritarianism and democracy as expressions of communal life. These two approaches to government don't move to the same beat.

Ultimately, we have to decide which type of dance we want to be a part of personally and what kinds of music will be allowed to play in our national dance hall so that others can enjoy their music, feel free to dance, and have their souls touched as well. Today's competing sounds define two fundamentally different ways of being in community with one another, and the one we choose will determine how we relate to others and the size and inclusivity of the dance floor we are willing to be a part of.

These music venues can be wonderful places to experience joy, individual creativity, celebration, and inclusion. But as the narrative revealed in the movie *West Side Story* reminds us, even with great, varied, award-winning music playing in the background, a dance floor can also be a place of conflict, unhealthy competition, prejudice, and even violence.

The struggle between these two dominating narratives raises several questions for me:

- How can I survive our current political situation and maintain a sense of spiritual rootedness, emotional stability, and hope for the future when so many of the values defining today's political realities are contrary to my core spiritual beliefs (i.e., the music that touches and moves my soul)?

- How can I make positive contributions to civic life when there is so much negativity, division, and cynicism in our society?

- What happens when those in power no longer want to govern for the good of an entire nation, inspiring the sense of domestic tranquility that the founders envisioned, but instead choose to rule our society for the benefit of the few?

These questions are what led me to write *Navigating Trumpworld*. If you are holding this book in your hands, I assume these are among the questions you are asking yourself as well.

This challenge is complicated further by the fact that it is difficult to both maintain a sense of integrity, utilizing one's voice and speaking one's truth freely, while at the same time remaining curious, receptive, and willing to listen to the variety of perspectives and realities that others live with. This is the dilemma of living in turbulent times such as ours.

And yet there may be a sense of hidden blessing buried here as well. After all, such a dynamic forces us all to go deeper spiritually in order to create the kind of democratic society that has always been a part of the American experiment that the founders hoped to create. *Navigating Trumpworld* has to do with speaking truth to power while also listening to others who we share community with so that together we can move to a healthier place spiritually. This is precisely the kind of community that Parker Palmer is referring to in the words above, where we can find our true selves in communities willing to embrace and include us all.

Until we get there, as the old expression goes, we're "in a heap of trouble." This starts with the fact that it is incredibly difficult to know how or even where to begin a conversation about politics in the United States today. People have such contrary views of what our reality actually is that it makes it hard to have meaningful conversations. This puts us at an immediate disadvantage in finding a way forward because it's hard to know how to proceed when you aren't able to talk about where you currently are, or to build common ground with each other.

Some among us are so outraged by the Trump administration's policies that it is difficult to even hear Donald Trump's name mentioned without getting upset, while others believe that President Trump is the best president we've had in recent memory. Many others just don't want to talk about politics anymore at all, and some aren't interested in political conversations because they don't think what is happening concerns them.

Wherever you find yourself on this spectrum, this book is an invitation to join in a conversation that will determine what kind of country we ultimately live in. With so many divergent views in play, it is challenging to make progress toward national unity, yet it is clear that tearing ourselves further apart will not serve us well in the end. These are confusing, stressful times that will require a great deal from all of us.

Over the past fifty years, I have been a local church pastor, as well as a church administrator, in rural, urban, and suburban communities. I have been a community organizer and program developer in a variety of settings, and I have worked across cultural boundaries frequently. In all those situations, I have met good, talented people who want to participate in civic life, work with others, and make their communities better places for everyone. There is no shortage of interest, talent, and ingenuity in this country, but currently we seem to be stuck with hostility, prejudices of one kind or another, and communal dysfunction and division.

Today, we are living in a significant historical moment in which Donald Trump and those who are a part of Trumpworld are in the process of undoing one hundred years of American history. They are doing this by undercutting public institutions and the social policies that have evolved over a long period of time and that undergird public trust, public consciousness, and public responsibility. These policies and institutions have served to define our commitment to each other as fellow Americans.

What makes this all the more difficult is that our defining qualities as Americans take place in the public square where our character, values, and spiritual life find their fullest expression. However, recent actions at the federal level have been articulated through disturbingly shallow public displays, involving character assassination, blatant materialism, and partisan political power, damaging the very qualities that help democracy succeed. In addition, there has been a noticeable void of public hearings and serious debate regarding many of the decisions that have been made. In the absence of such democratic norms, you are left with governance by the few, for the few.

As Richard Haass writes in his book *The Bill of Obligations: The Ten Habits of Good Citizens*, the results from this impact not only our country but the future of democracy throughout the world as well: "A country at war with itself cannot set an example that people elsewhere will want to emulate. If democracy fails here, democracy will be endangered everywhere."[1]

Whatever happens next, it will take years of conscientious investment and a renewed commitment to higher spiritual values to recover what has already been lost. Yes, we live in a significant, historical moment, and we have an important part to play in the outcome.

On one level, given the situation we find ourselves in today, this book could be characterized as being a call to arms, but in reality, it's more of a rallying cry directed at hearts. It isn't so much an appeal to become superhuman as it is a plea to be fully human. Now isn't a time for more Trumpworld grievance politics, which inevitably fosters suspicion, hostility, and revenge; it's time to be part of a national movement directed toward healing and renewal, which is grounded in compassion and shaped by curiosity and an openness to understanding and valuing others.

So, what happens next and what can we do?

1. Haass, *Bill of Obligations*, xii.

It begins by making a decision to return to basic, spiritual principles and develop a willingness to engage fully in our sociopolitical reality to see where we fit in the larger picture of things. We each have a role to play in turning chaos and cruelty into conversation and civility. As I will discuss later in practice 10, we must be participants, rather than bystanders, in community life.

This means we need to begin where we are. There are many circumstances that take place at a personal level that have nothing to do with political decisions or public policies but are a part of our social environment nonetheless. These situations and our responses to them impact what happens next because they occur within our own orbit of influence. For example:

- Have you ever witnessed someone making a racist or sexist comment in a group of people, but no one said anything in response?

- Have you ever observed an adult berate a child in public in a manner that felt troublesome, uncomfortable, or wrong, but you didn't know what to do?

- Have you ever worked in a situation in which a boss demeaned a fellow employee, and you felt helpless to do anything about it for fear that this boss' wrath might be taken out on you?

- Have you ever seen a public altercation or road rage situation between two individuals and wondered what happened later?

Cruelty in any form is a troubling thing to witness. Yet, these situations happen in our world all too frequently. It's disconcerting whenever you find yourself in the role of being a bystander to some form of inhumane behavior and remain silent or can't figure out how to participate in a constructive manner. Private suffering is incredibly lonely. Being on the end of unjustified or cruel public dealings causes deep trauma to individuals and can alter the atmosphere of an entire community, destroying its social cohesion.

When such things occur, a key question to ask yourself is this: Is a person being harmed—physically, emotionally, or spiritually—as a result of what is taking place? If they are, there is good reason to try and interfere in some manner, to change the flow of energy, to resist the injustice that you are witnessing. Of course, each situation requires a different response, but in the end, what can you do to lessen the harm being done?

We cannot always change the course of cruelty when we see it, but if we allow it to go unchecked, over time such cruelty will change us and the communities we live in.

I have thought a great deal about what watching public displays of inhumanity means in recent years as I've observed Donald Trump and those in his inner circle. On numerous occasions, his insulting public comments and actions have diminished the human spirit and harmed others in very real ways.

And this list continues to grow. I can't help but think about the time when Donald Trump made fun of a person with disabilities in front of the press or when he threw packages of paper towels to hurricane victims in Puerto Rico during his first administration. Of course, he still continues to use name-calling as a way of insulting or punishing those he wants to get even with. And we're not even talking about the very real impact that his public policy decisions have had on those affected by his actions.

As his second administration begins, President Trump has escalated such behaviors in a dramatic fashion and has changed the lives of hundreds of thousands of people. In addition to being publicly demeaned, people have lost their jobs, been deported, had their federal grants withdrawn, and lost their social status within society. Such actions are neither civil nor life-giving and are contrary to the essence of the American spirit. Tragically, in many ways, President Trump has normalized this kind of behavior on a global scale.

But as my mom used to say when I was young and someone acted inappropriately in public, "That's really not necessary. People are capable of being better than that." Everyone is able to do great good if they choose to do so. There is no reason to hurt others when people can be better served with more thoughtful and compassionate actions. This has been my experience throughout life.

The truth is, Trump's way doesn't represent how most people behave toward others. However, when he does hurtful, even illegal, things, it is difficult not to find oneself getting distressed and feeling like a bystander since Trump's actions are so far removed from our personal circles of influence. Yet, his actions impact our entire society in significant and long-lasting ways.

If it weren't for the fact that President Trump is doing so much damage to the lives of so many innocent people, I would feel sorry for the man. As small-spirited as many of his actions are, Donald Trump is still a human being, and it's clear that anyone involved in these kinds of behaviors is a deeply troubled, insecure, unhappy, wounded human being.

It's hard to know what happened in his life to push Trump to be so insensitive and hostile. But nothing occurs in a vacuum, which makes one wonder: Was he unloved as a child? Does he have an unhappy marriage? Has he become increasingly unfulfilled, realizing that for all his wealth and power, he isn't really a joyful person? Perhaps he never studied the great spiritual traditions of the world, so he doesn't know any other way to behave and lacks the inner resources to change course.

Mary Trump, Donald's niece, looks at a number of factors involved in her uncle's behaviors in her revealing book *Too Much and Never Enough*, pointing out that the "casual dehumanization of people was commonplace at the Trump dinner table."[2] As we discuss in practice 4, if the feelings related to this dehumanization of people have not been transformed in his life, then most assuredly, this explains why Donald Trump continues to transmit negative feelings toward others. It is a kind of contagion that is released in the world and impacts people years later as it continues to be passed on.

No matter what undergirds his actions, in the end Trump and Trumpworld have not only become an American phenomenon, but this reality is now taking aim at the essence of America's historic and democratic ideals.

---

2. Trump, *Too Much and Never Enough*, 9.

Our founders—Washington, Hamilton, Madison, Franklin, Adams, Jefferson, et al.—were well-versed in the philosophies and traditions involved with character development. They understood, through their study of ancient Greek and Roman societies, how character influenced public life. And as a result, they were deeply suspicious of the potential abuse of power and the temptations that authoritarian rule posed to a democratic society.

Individuals are capable of great good but also of great evil. Because of this, the founders were concerned about how power could be used by leaders within a society, and they would clearly be alarmed by what is taking place in the United States today.

Trumpworld involves both an undeveloped, compromised sense of ancient character values combined with a clear set of policy strategies that together take aim at the essence of what America is on our best days, as well as undercutting how we portray ourselves to the rest of the world.

The reality is that Trumpworld, for all its clarity, is still a work in progress. Project 2025 is pretty explicit, and many of its policy initiatives have already been put into place. There are many things we know now about where public policies are headed and what kind of worldview is being created, but commentators are still struggling to define what it all means and where it will take us in the end. Without question, this journey will continue to be an interplay between the qualities of character and the results they produce within society.

Consider the writer William Cooper, for example. In April 2025, he said, "So we find ourselves today charting new territory as a nation. Some parts of our democracy still work, some don't, and some of our fears have been realized. We are not under the yoke of a fascist dictator. We are, rather, neck-deep in the dysfunctional scramble of a constitutionally illiterate and shameless bully."[3]

In Germany in the early 1930s, something similar could have been written as fascism entered the scene. It was a relatively new phenomenon at the time, and Hitler's Germany was not the same as Mussolini's Italy. Each historical moment has its own unique

---

3. Cooper, "Four Pillars of Trumpism," A7.

distinctions. So, with Trumpworld, we are witnessing something entirely new and different, and yet, there is absolute clarity about its authoritarian and dictatorial dimensions. It is about one man's vision for the future of his nation combined with an unwillingness to consider the viewpoints of our rich and varied nation.

The uncertainty that Trump and Trumpworld creates within the American body politic is deeply disturbing and has caused not only tremendous stress to our political system but also a great deal of uncertainty in the lives of countless people. What is certain and what is fleeting? What reflects our deeply held values and what is just part of the latest negotiation? The current situation makes it difficult to build trust, form community, and plan for the future. One wonders if this is part of Trumpworld's game plan for the country. It is difficult to maintain democratic norms when everything is in a state of constant flux.

As a result, it is not surprising that according to the World Happiness Report for 2025, of the 147 nations listed in the report, the United States has dropped to twenty-fourth on the happiness scale.[4] This position reflects the lowest ranking we've ever held in this global analysis as a country.

For all our wealth and material prosperity, for all our pride in our American personal freedom, we simply don't appear to be a terribly happy people when we are compared to other nations. While this may not be as materially easy to track as stock market numbers or our gross national product (GNP), our lack of happiness as a people is cause for concern.

While it may be true that happiness without freedom is ultimately an illusion, it is also true that freedom without happiness doesn't lead to a sense of lasting satisfaction, nor does it create the kind of community that reflects our highest human values.

So, how did we get here and what does it mean for our future? There are a lot of contributing factors involved, and increasingly those factors are reflected in the daily news:

- Immigrants deported without due process.

4. Helliwell et al., *World Happiness Report 2025*, 17.

- Government workers abruptly fired without cause.
- The free press attacked for having differing policy opinions or asking unwelcome questions.
- Historic allies insulted, demeaned, and considered trade enemies rather than international partners.
- The federal government reneging on its contract obligations and defunding public agencies.
- Issues related to hunger, public health, and education unfunded and set aside.

It's time to take a closer look at what is occurring in the United States and determine not only how to navigate our current situation but also figure out what role we can play in altering the outcome. The struggle is not simply about differences of opinion regarding public policies. That is normal. More importantly, it is about our drift toward despotism, the undermining of our humanity, the diminishment of public spaces, and the impact this has on our collective spirituality.

When Sinclair Lewis wrote *It Can't Happen Here* in 1935, he was warning Americans then about the fragility of democracy and the possibility that fascism could take hold here. In his book, Lewis demonstrates how it can happen in the United States by writing about the rise of a president who becomes the leader of the country in order to save it from welfare cheats, sex, crime, and the liberal press. In Lewis's novel, Buzz Windrip becomes an American dictator.

As Lewis points out, people should have seen it coming since at one point, candidate Windrip promotes his "Fifteen Points of Victory for the Forgotten Men" in which point fifteen reads,

> Congress shall, immediately upon our inauguration, initiate amendments to the Constitution providing (a) that the President shall have the authority to institute and execute all necessary measures for the conduct of the government during this critical epoch; (b) that Congress shall serve only in an advisory capacity, calling to the attention of the President and his aides and Cabinet

any needed legislation, but not acting upon same until authorized by the President so to act; and (c) that the Supreme Court shall immediately have removed from its jurisdiction the power to negate, by ruling them to be unconstitutional or by any other judicial action, any or all acts of the President, his duly appointed aides or Congress.[5]

Given what has been happening in the United States in recent days, reading *It Can't Happen Here* nearly a hundred years after it was first published sounds eerily familiar.

All you have to do is add immigrants, federal workers, and those who support diversity, inclusion, and equity to the mix and you've cooked up a fresh, new batch of American-style fascism.

Fascism depends on creating divisions within a nation and putting people down in order to be successful. When this happens, it creates a kind of faux power among people, in which individuals feel like they have a voice and a sense of agency, yet collectively they don't have any real power at all. Lewis put it this way in his book: "Every man is a king so long as he has someone to look down on."[6] This attitude requires a shift in a person's spiritual life so that one's personal gain and sense of fulfillment depends on someone else's pain. The Trump administration is effectively using this approach, but it is not the basis upon which a democracy is built.

What we are witnessing today is a battle between two distinct and contrasting views of government continually clashing with each other. This conflict represents what the American founders were dealing with when they created the American democratic experiment over two centuries ago and tried to establish a better form of government that took into account the variety of individuals who lived within their society.

I think about these two different approaches to governing as representing my experience of buying a new pair of shoes. There are many choices to consider. Some brands seem to work for me. Others not so much. What I've come to realize over the years is

5. Lewis, *It Can't Happen Here*, 64.
6. Lewis, *It Can't Happen Here*, 157.

that certain shoe brands have soles that interact with the unique shape of my foot and create the right kind of space I need in order to walk pain free, while others are more rigid, sometimes either being too structured and confining or lacking in adequate support, forcing my foot to fit into their preconceived design.

Ultimately, there has to be enough flexibility in the design of the shoe so that my foot can fit and I can walk with comfort. The outcome is a matter of design. What is the right amount of structure? What is the right amount of space and support needed for each unique foot—mine included? In some ways the soul of a nation and the sole of a shoe are similar in this way—both need to interact with those involved in such a way that everyone involved can walk freely and without unnecessary suffering.

The viewpoint the founders were attacking in the late 1700s was based on one that today we'd consider to be authoritarian or dictatorial. For them, this had to do with monarchy and the dominating influence of a colonial power—the few had the power, and the many were without adequate representation. They were trying to create the right mix of personal freedom and political structure so they could create the kind of country worth fighting for and those involved could walk freely with just the right amount of support and structure—a well-designed equilibrium between rights and obligations, checks and balances.

When power constricts, those with power have the ability to dictate what life looks like for the many. In other words, the king knows best. A distant authority makes the rules. And power is used to determine who gets what, who has rights, and who has a place and/or voice at the table. Literally, one shoe designed to fit all, even if it causes pain and discomfort to many. How this equation plays out determines what kind of government you are a part of.

Our founders saw government as being an important part of community life. It was to be a positive resource designed to embrace the natural competing voices of the many so that "we the people" could work through our differences via civic institutions in order to create agreeable public policies. The foundation of this form of government was to include representation from the many, not to restrict, exclude, or repress those who were to be governed. It was to take the form of a representative democracy. Abraham Lincoln articulated this same vision years later at Gettysburg, saying that it was to be a government of, by, and for the people.

However, it is important to note that from the beginning the founders themselves had a limited understanding of what "we the people" meant, since those who were enslaved and the voices of women were not a part of their eighteenth-century understanding of "we." Nonetheless, they did have the foresight to understand that unchecked power was dangerous and could ultimately be tyrannical.

It's not that what is taking place today is completely new, but what is taking place is an attempt to institutionalize our country's prior authoritarian tendencies and make them central to how our government operates and develops policy.

This became increasingly clear to me when I read the news about individuals being detained by ICE in their communities or at airports in the United States. It was a chilling reminder of something I personally witnessed in the San Salvador airport in El Salvador in 1981, at the height of the repression there.

While making an airplane change in that country, I saw armed Salvadoran military personnel select several individuals from the waiting area and take them into offices located behind opaque glass. Knowing what was taking place in the prisons of El Salvador at the time made me very uneasy but also grateful that I was an American and presumably safe from such things. And yet, in recent days, individuals on American soil have been forcibly detained and sent to some of those Salvadoran prisons nearly fifty years later without due process or legal representation. These actions have become part of official administration policy and represent what our public image is to the rest of the world.

How do we respond as Americans when this reality finally sinks in? After all, authoritarianism does not take place all at once, nor does it affect people equally. Authoritarianism generally rolls out unevenly, making those on the margins victims long before taking on those who have enough power to resist what is happening. On the surface, everything seems to be fine, unless you happen to be directly affected. Then, at some point in time, all the pieces come together, and everyone is impacted in one way or another.

I'll never forget going to the United States Holocaust Memorial Museum in Washington, DC, years ago for the first time. I was stunned when I got off the elevator to enter the first exhibit area. It wasn't filled with a huge mound of shoes from those who had been killed in the gas ovens or photographs of prisoners at Auschwitz, Treblinka, Buchenwald, or Dachau.

Instead, the beginning of the exhibit included a series of glass cases and wall displays filled with the historical documents that chronicled the rise of fascism in Germany in the 1930s before the concentration and death camps were established and millions were killed. This museum display was a horrifying and important reminder that political viewpoints were set in motion and policy decisions took place in Nazi Germany long before the "final solution" was implemented and people lost their freedom and/or were killed. One thing could not have happened without the other.

Mind you, I'm not predicting massive arrests or the creation of concentration camps on this kind of scale in the United States, but it did make me think about the recently repurposed detention center at Guantanamo Bay and El Salvador's acceptance of American deportees as an unusual way of treating people who were simply trying to immigrate to the United States.

Both destinations have a dark, secret quality to them and reflect the Trump administration's clever way of ramping up their deportation policy without anyone having the opportunity to ask questions about their actions or challenge the legality of what is taking place. And if you are not involved, it is easy to ignore what is happening. One might say, "Out of sight, out of mind."

Emerging authoritarianism always works like this: Some lose their voice first, then others. Some aren't seen or valued, then others. Some are deprived of their personal power, then others.

In other words, while it has been easy to deport immigrants without cause previously, now it is possible for those who work for the federal government to be fired abruptly, those who do research that the new government no longer supports to lose their federal grants, and those who refuse to go along with the Trump administration's agenda to be attacked publicly. These individuals and their families have already experienced what a dictatorship feels like, and there is a human cost involved that impacts all of us.

And yet, in the midst of such actions, there are those who not only agree with what is taking place but don't understand why anyone would be upset about what is occurring. These individuals are fellow citizens, and many are our neighbors. In a democracy, people are free to make their own choices, but this is also how authoritarianism works its way into the body politic.

It functions like a type of cancer that first roots itself within the anatomy in those places where it can gain a foothold before it metastasizes and spreads throughout the rest of the body. While it remains present, however, the cancer weakens everyone's overall immunity and makes the rest of the body more susceptible to other diseases.

This is what has been taking place in the United States over the past decade. Trumpworld didn't take root all at once. It needed willing hosts first, who welcomed its values and practices into their lives, before it could spread on a larger scale. Now it has become a dominant American reality and is having an impact on the entire nation.

While it has evolved over time, Trumpworld can no longer simply be confined to the notion of "Make America Great Again" (MAGA, for short). It is much more than that. Deep down it hinges on the proclivities, pathologies, and personality of Donald Trump. He gives this movement its foundation, and he continues to be its primary spokesperson. Without Donald Trump, it is fair to say that there would be no Trumpworld. But that is not to say there would be no fascist tendencies in America. They would simply take on another form.

Trump 1.0, from 2016 to 2020, was filled with drama and chaos that focused on building the wall along our southern border, often resulting in children being separated from their parents in the process; tax cuts that favored those with wealth; the elimination of various kinds of federal regulation; increased government support for the fossil fuel industry; bilateral global agreements being valued more than multilateral agreements and historic alliances; and attempts to repeal or undercut the Affordable Care Act.

Trump 2.0 has only been in place a short time, but already it has demonstrated that things will lead to a very different outcome. Using Project 2025 as a guide and playbook, this Trump administration still has high drama, but now it is focused, strategic, and unrelenting, undercutting well-established American democratic principles in record time. Already, some have indicated that nearly 50 percent of Project 2025's recommendations have been put in place. A remarkable achievement given the fact that candidate Trump said he knew nothing about Project 2025 and hadn't read it.

In Trump 1.0, there was an attempt to acquire expansive power. In Trump 2.0, there is a conscious desire to consolidate executive power in a dangerous and authoritarian manner.

What this means in reality is that tens of thousands of immigrants have been deported, thousands of federal workers have been fired from their jobs, birthright citizenship is being challenged, people are being picked up by ICE agents and taken away in unmarked cars, abortion rights and maternal and child services are being curtailed, the US military and Homeland Security have seen their roles expand, the Department of Education is being dismantled, the courts and free press have been attacked, and historic American economic and military alliances have been dismantled as tariffs and assorted insults have become a regular part of American foreign policy. This will result in less government and less regulation but also in less democratic oversight and fewer voices being involved in the formation of our national identity.

So, how did we get here exactly?

Some would say it all began with the self-indulgence of the 1960s and the numerous assassinations of key civic leaders who were a part of that era; others, that it has to do with the rise of Christian nationalism and the growth of anti-government militias. Still others would say that President Carter saw it coming when he made his famous "malaise" speech in 1979 and spoke about the "crisis in confidence" that he saw happening in the United States, while for others it has to do with the anti-government sentiments that were at the core of the Reagan Revolution and were expressed best in 1986 when President Reagan said, "The nine most terrifying words in the English language are: I'm from the government, and I'm here to help," effectively undercutting the role and value of those involved in public service.[7]

Of course, Newt Gingrich's "Contract with America," the rise of the Tea Party Movement, and Mitch McConnell's long tenure as majority leader in the Senate serve as additional guideposts along the way.

For me, I saw the early signs of what has led us to Trumpworld in the mid-1980s when I moved from the San Francisco Bay Area to Filer, Idaho (population: fifteen hundred). That move taught me a great deal about the growing gap between our different, disconnected realities as a country and our inability to understand people who weren't from where we come from. It ultimately has to do with having a lack of curiosity, which naturally leads to a sense of disconnection between people.

During those years, whenever I'd return to visit the Bay Area, a number of friends were dumbfounded that I had moved from paradise to the middle of nowhere, in their view. It was as if I had left earth and relocated to another planet. What was I thinking?

When I talked to people in Filer about San Francisco, often I'd get a look as if to say, "I bet you're glad you got out of that place with all its traffic, urbanization, and social problems."

In both locales, I met wonderful people who cared about their families, worked hard, and tried to make the world a better place. It was a reminder that there are conscientious people living everywhere. On one level, both places often seemed to those living there to be the center of the world. Sometimes it was hard for many of them to understand why people would want to live anyplace else. Yet, frequently I'd say, "You'd be surprised by how

7. Reagan, "News Conference."

much you have in common." I'm not sure what folks in either place thought about that declaration, but it was true.

However, one incident has always stood out as a reminder of how easy it is to create barriers rather than connections between us when we lack curiosity and empathy. It happened one day when I left Filer for a meeting across the Snake River Canyon in Jerome. Jerome is located twenty-three miles north and approximately thirty minutes from Filer, but you have to go to Twin Falls, which is located to the east of Filer, in order to reach the bridge that takes you across the canyon.

That afternoon, when I returned home, I attended a meeting at someone's house in the community and told them where I had been, closing by saying, "I'm sure you've been to Jerome many times before."

To my surprise, the person I was talking to said in so many words that no, she had never been to Jerome before. When I asked her why, she simply said, "Why would I go to Jerome when everything I need is here in Filer?"

This question has always served as a kind of metaphor for me regarding curiosity and the art of living in the world. I've often pondered this statement, wondering what it reveals about the human condition. Without wanting to be overly judgmental, I've tried to understand why this individual wasn't at least interested enough in going to Jerome in order to see the canyon from the other side and get a different perspective of her own town from there. After all, it's impossible to see the entire landscape from any one location.

Today, this is about more than where you live physically. Now, we are surrounded by countless echo chambers—virtual locales, if you will—that keep us primarily situated in one place, whether this be the result of refusing to venture out from our favorite podcast, FOX, MSNBC, CNN, or a host of other virtual places that can dominate our lives and shape our worldviews. Unless we are interested and willing to venture out, traverse the nearest bridge, and cross the canyon that separates us from other folks, we'll end up in a similar place as my friend that afternoon in Filer without even knowing it.

This can easily take a dark turn when a lack of curiosity becomes filled with negativity, blame, and judgment. Negativity is incredibly seductive because it allows a person to complain and blame others without doing the hard work of inner spiritual reflection.

Whatever the case, one could say that a number of signs during the past fifty years have foreshadowed where we currently are, and that the tide of authoritarian rule and oligarchy has been evolving long before settling in the form of Trumpworld. This has happened because of the habits, practices, and patterns we've developed in our lives and country over a number of years.

One of the significant differences today, however, is that Trumpworld is not only promoting negativity, blame, and judgment toward others in dangerous ways while advancing a new version of authoritarianism in American garb, but it is also undoing the history of public progress that has been made in the United States during the past fifty-plus years.

This progress has involved expanding voting rights, human rights, health care options, and care for child and elders, among other things. Undoing such historic achievements is painful to see because progress in democratic societies is slow. But as we are experiencing, our progress can be reversed quickly when someone who has despotic inclinations seizes control of the levers of power.

When authoritarianism is successful, it eventually becomes synonymous with one individual, not with the diversity and collective qualities of an entire nation. This means that as the moods and manners of one person change, so too does the direction of an entire country.

When Donald Trump declared in his March 2025 address to Congress that "America won't be woke anymore" and proceeded to sign executive orders removing all diversity, equity, and inclusion policies across the federal government and encouraged the same things to take place within the private sector, he didn't mention that the opposite of diversity is sameness and uniformity, that the opposite of equity is injustice, partiality, prejudice, and unfairness, and that the opposite of inclusion is exclusion.

Those are the qualities that are often used to describe the impact of authoritarianism on a society. But Donald Trump would prefer that we not read the fine print that describes the kind of world he is creating when he declares that we will be "woke" no more.

So, among other things, Trump's attacks on DEI not only eliminated a number of people's jobs without any form of due process, but by eliminating all efforts to focus on our country's diversity, concerns related to equity, and the value of inclusion, he effectively made our national focus be one that supports uniformity, injustice, and exclusion.

It reminds me of a sermon I heard preached years ago at All Souls Unitarian Church in Washington, DC. The pastor was speaking at a national conference that included people from across the United States. He wanted those attending to understand the history of his church—about the diversity of the people who attended there, the various causes the congregation had supported over the years, and why the name All Souls was so important.

At one point, the pastor said that it made a difference that his church was called All Souls, after all who would want to attend a church named "Some Souls." He went on to say that as far as he knew, there were no churches actually named "Some Souls," even though a number of congregations acted toward others as if there were only some souls that were truly valued.

He said he didn't believe this was the way of Jesus, who reached out to people of all types and stations in life, told parables about cross-cultural interactions, and included women in his inner circle at a time when prejudices against women and those from other cultures were common.

Today, by eliminating the fundamental practices of diversity, equity, and inclusion from our government, Donald Trump has said in no uncertain terms that he believes in a "Some Souls" country. This approach to governing a nation does not represent the high-water mark that has served as an inspiration for countless people over the years. Is a "Some Souls" society really what will Make America Great Again?

These are not normal times. You hear people say this frequently today. And usually, when these words are spoken, they describe something negative. What we are experiencing today is not normal, nor does it frame an encouraging picture of the future. Instead, many things taking place today constitute an assault on the fundamental assumptions of a democratic society and question the existential nature of our social life as a people.

But Ben Rhodes points out in his book *After the Fall* that what is happening in the United States today is occurring within the context of a larger, global movement that embraces authoritarianism, with Viktor Orban, Hungary's prime minister, serving as a textbook example.

Rhodes says that our version of this global movement shares a number of tendencies with other authoritarian expressions: "In America, as in Hungary, the right wing has embraced a nationalism characterized by Christian identity, national sovereignty, distrust of democratic institutions, opposition to immigration, and contempt for politically correct liberal elites."[8] He goes on to say that this approach depends on an "us versus them" paradigm that favors some but clearly is not open to all.

A lot is at stake, and much is required of us. In his book *On Tyranny*, Timothy Snyder says, "In founding a democratic republic upon law and establishing a system of checks and balances, the Founding Fathers sought to avoid the evil that they, like the ancient philosophers, called tyranny. They had in mind the usurpation of power by a single individual or group, or the circumvention of law by rulers for their own benefit."[9]

It is hard to believe what has happened in recent months in the United States has led us in the direction of tyranny in which an individual and group has circumvented the law in order to benefit themselves, but we are where we are, and now it is up to us to do something about it.

8. Rhodes, *After the Fall*, 35.
9. Synder, *On Tyranny*, 9–10.

Not since the civil rights movement of the 1950s and 1960s has our nation faced a time such as this. Of course, one might say, "But what about 9/11?"

The difference between September 11, 2001, when the attacks on the Twin Towers in New York City took place, and what we are experiencing today is clear and simple: the former was an attack from outside our country that was a violent assault against our nation that resulted in the killing of several thousand innocent people, which required our collective, unified response.

The emergence of Trumpworld represents something quite different. It is first and foremost a spiritual, existential assault on our identity as a democracy and on our sense of human decency and kindness. In this case, what threatens our future is being initiated from within our national borders, not from some foreign adversary. Yet, it has already had a profound impact on all of us, and we are not done with things yet.

Increasingly, political commentators are drawing the connections between the Trump administration's formation of policies and the public use of callousness and cruelty toward others. In an April 2025 commentary on a number of public policy decisions, Tom Moran wrote, "Why does a man who cultivates such cruelty still have the support of nearly half the country? In the end, that question may be just as important."[10]

In order to answer this question, it will require us to do some serious spiritual work ourselves, and that begins by developing a different, more humane, and civil way of being in relationship with each other.

---

10. Moran, "Trump's Unbound Cruelty," A11.

A Reader's Guide

Where Do We Go from Here?

The time has come, God knows, for us to examine ourselves, but we can only do this if we are willing to free ourselves of the myth of America and try to find out what is really happening here.

—James Baldwin

NAVIGATING TRUMPWORLD IS MADE up of twelve distinct spiritual insights and practices, which have all been negatively impacted by Trumpworld's perspective and policies. At the same time, these same twelve practices can serve as resources of resilience and resistance as we work to create a safer, more civil, and just society.

Before proceeding, however, it is necessary to make an important disclaimer. Since we live in such a diverse and complex world, not everyone fits into neat packages or embodies the stereotypes, generalizations, or assumptions we often make about those who see the world differently than we do. We are each distinct and unique human beings, after all.

This is true of what I am calling "Trumpworld" as well. Not everyone involved comes to this worldview in the same manner, nor is every "Trumper" responsible for all the policies and behaviors that result from what is happening. The ingredients that are a part of the current, prevailing American stew consist of a large number of different, unique individuals. Yet, while Donald Trump and his closest associates may be the cooks in the kitchen who are stirring the pot and doing the most harm, at some point, those who follow along and support what is taking place have some responsibility for the outcomes we are experiencing.

So, for example, while thousands of people participated in the events of January 6, 2021, not everyone who was involved did so for the same reason, and not everyone present committed criminal acts. Some clearly were engaged in violence, the desecration of public property and violence and harm being done to others, while undoubtedly a number of people who were there thought they were participating in a raucous political rally that simply got way out of control.

Some of those present needed to go to jail, while others just needed to go home. Not everyone committed crimes against others, but at the same time, not everyone who was sent to prison for the crimes they committed should have been pardoned in a universal manner. The reality is that everyone who went to jail received due process. In the end, the cumulative perspectives represented on January 6 did great damage to the political and spiritual fabric of the nation.

My point is this: generalizations are dicey. They can do great harm in and of themselves and slow the healing and community-building process. And yet, it is important to be clear and concise about both innocence and wrongdoing while also confronting harm and injustice forthrightly when you see it taking place. This is what I am attempting to do in *Navigating Trumpworld*.

So, when I speak of Trumpworld in the following pages, I am well aware that this group of individuals includes Christian nationalists and social conservatives, evangelicals and libertarians, white supremacists and independents, and lots of people like my own neighbors, who I talk with on a regular basis about a variety of things, including family, sports, cars, work, and other things of mutual interest. A number of them are a part of Trumpworld, but they have done no great crimes, nor should they be demonized for their beliefs. Like all of us, they are simply trying to understand

and participate in our democratic society given the resources at their disposal.

In short, Trumpworld is not a one-size-fits-all phenomenon. But those who are opposed to what is happening at the hands of the Trumpworld and those who are the targets of Trumpworld do not constitute a single monolith either. They do not deserve to be treated as being less than human beings with rights and responsibilities of their own. This includes immigrants, federal workers, social advocates, those receiving Medicaid, those advocating for diversity, equity, and inclusion, those seeking abortions, public school teachers, progressives, and people like me. Like those in Trumpworld, we too have voices that need to be heard.

This reality complicates our ability to find common ground. That will take time and lots of listening, conversations, second questions, storytelling, curiosity, mutual interest, and understanding. This is an important part of the analysis and conversation that we are involved in, and there are a number of important guides who can help us in that venture. They include: Mónica Guzmán (*I Never Thought of It That Way*), Michelle Norris (*Our Hidden Conversations*), Mark Yaconelli (*Between the Listening and the Telling*), and Sherry Turkle (*Reclaiming Conversation*), among many others. This is at the heart of the work that is ahead of us.

That said, living in the all-consuming world of Donald Trump is exhausting. It seems almost impossible to escape his influence. Trump not only plays a significant role in politics, he also enters into the world of the arts, higher education, pop culture, sports, and anywhere else where he feels the need to dictate the outcome to his liking. This is what authoritarians do—they make their presence known everywhere.

While this is deeply disturbing and profoundly undemocratic in nature, it does not have to be the end of the story. We all have a part to play in what happens next, and spirituality is at the heart of this alternative narrative.

On a personal note, in response to what is unfolding today, I don't want my spiritual life to be sabotaged in such a way that my outward actions no longer reflect my highest inner values. This is a valid concern given the negativity, cynicism, and chaos that increasingly seeps into everyday American life.

Instead, I want my inner spirit to be a reservoir from which I am able to make positive contributions in the world. It is a natural part of a well-grounded spiritual life that will be discussed further in practice 1.

The United States is currently experiencing a kind of spiritual schizophrenia, which is dividing us politically and damaging the soul of the nation. Who are we really? And what kind of people do we want to be?

These basic questions get at the crux of the matter. Are we a kind, generous, compassionate people capable of making the world a better place and representing "a shining city on a hill," as President Reagan so often declared? Or, have we sunk to our lowest common denominator spiritually and now resent others, seek revenge, and aren't interested in matters of fairness, equality, and justice anymore? The answer to these questions can be found in the quality of our inner lives, the sense of character we develop, and the social expressions that come from the values we cultivate.

Spirituality can be defined in a number of ways. It has to do with one's conscience, moral compass, inner voice, soul. It speaks to one's essence, deepest values, the so-called God spot within. One's inner spirit is what anchors our outer universe and serves as the center of our lives. It would be fair to say that spirituality is the sun around which everything else revolves. Everyone has something that grounds how they think about life and how they live on a daily basis.

Howard Thurman referred to this place as "the island of peace within one's soul," saying it is the spot within us that defines who we are and is the place where plans are made. It is from this place that one's life moves forward. In light of this, Thurman says, "How foolish it is, how terrible, if you have not found your Island of Peace within your own soul! It means that you are living without the discovery of your true home."[1]

---

1. Thurman, *Meditations of the Heart*, 18.

So, what do you do when the things you value most in life—honesty and integrity, compassion and kindness, curiosity and scientific exploration, understanding and justice, patience and humility, inclusion and community, diversity and the free expression of various cultural traditions, and equity and fairness—are not valued by those in power, nor do they play a central role in the public policy decisions being undertaken by those with wealth and position?

At first glance, it makes you want to react and resist however you can. But before doing so, it is vitally important to pause, step back, and ask yourself some fundamental questions:

- What do I value most and how are those values demonstrated in my life?

- How do I want to practice those values when living in a hostile environment?

- How does living our values impact those around us? Do they promote good or do they do harm to others?

- How do I want to spend my time and energy?

- Who are we and what do we want to become as a society? And what role can I play within this bigger picture?

- What kind of world do I want to pass on to my children and grandchildren?

In order to get at these questions, we must not only look around us at matters of public policy and social behaviors but dig a bit deeper as well into our inner thoughts, words, and the metaphors we live by. This will help us determine what values shape our worldview and ultimately determine the practices that become central to our lives.

This reminds me of a story that Samuel Dresner shares about an encounter he had with the great Jewish rabbi and theologian Abraham Heschel, following a near fatal heart attack Heschel experienced in 1972.

Dresner describes how when he visited Heschel shortly after this event, Heschel told him that when he regained consciousness, he felt gratitude rather than despair or anger. Heschel went on to say how many miracles he had seen in his lifetime and then said, "That is what I meant when I wrote (in the preface to his book of Yiddish poems): 'I did not ask for success; I asked for wonder. And You gave it to me.'"[2]

It was wonder that Heschel most valued, and it is in this light that he saw the world.

How different this is from the "Trumpian" worldview that is based on suspicion, resentment, certainty, and hostility.

"I wonder" opens the world up to its rich diversity in an inclusive manner. Suspicion leads to an understanding that nothing good can come from this. One is an expression that leads toward a democratic instinct; the other is filled with authoritarian overtones. In either case, what is valued most determines both personal and social patterns, and patterns turn into behaviors. This leads us back to the wisdom that Heschel has to share.

In an interview that took place ten days before Heschel died, the interviewer asked him if there was any message that he'd like to share with young people. Heschel responded, saying, "Remember that there is meaning beyond absurdity. Know that every deed counts, that every word is power. . . . Above all, remember that you must build your life as if it were a work of art."[3]

As I will describe in practice 1, life flows in an inward-out manner, so what goes on inside of us matters a great deal. Deeds count. Words are power. Our lives matter, but that happens from inside out. This is where our muses and demons do battle with each other and where we shape our inner spirits and form our outer lives.

It is also the nexus where Trumpworld meets those who believe in democracy and where these forces engage each other to determine the kind of world we live in. It is also where words are either used as weapons or tools for exploration, where others

2. Dresner, introduction to *I Asked for Wonder*, vii.

3. Dresner, introduction to *I Asked for Wonder*, ix.

are either approached or feared, where the metaphors one chooses shape the world one sees, and where communities are formed or barriers are constructed.

George Lakoff and Mark Johnson explore the power of language in their timeless book *Metaphors We Live By*, and they invite us into understanding how our stories, thoughts, and words define us:

> Imagine a culture where an argument is viewed as a dance, the participants are seen as performers, and the goal is to perform in a balanced and aesthetically pleasing way. In such a culture, people would view arguments differently, experience them differently, carry them out differently, and talk about them differently.[4]

They go on to say that the metaphors we embrace shape how we see the world, and how we see the world defines our everyday realities.

This book is an attempt to invite you into a dance with spiritual metaphors and foundational inner values in the hope that you will find the resources you need to not only navigate Trumpworld but find a pathway forward in which you can join others to create an effective democratic resistance. Together we can bring about the healing and health we need to return our country to our founding ideals and a place of greater social wholeness.

Today, many individuals are finding themselves in dramatically different situations than they anticipated being in. When this happens, it is shocking and destabilizing.

- Imagine being told, "You're fired," for no apparent, logical, or performance-related reason, even though you've worked for the government for years and perhaps even served your country in the armed forces. How would you feel?

- Imagine being told that you and your family must leave the country or you are detained by ICE officials even though you were born in the United States. What would you do?

4. Lakoff and Johnson, *Metaphors We Live By*, 5.

- Imagine you were about to have a baby but couldn't find the proper maternal and child health care that you needed. Or what if you knew about family history that included stories of the ravages of polio or measles, but you lived in a community where these medical services and protections were no longer available? What questions would you ask those with the power to decide these things?

At some point, you'd undoubtedly wonder what kind of country you were living in and want to do something about it. But even if you have not experienced such drastic situations as these, it is quite likely that you have been impacted by some form of Trump-world cruelty, even if that means simply witnessing its impact on someone else.

This is when grounding ourselves in essential spiritual practices and finding others who have similar values and experiences is so vitally important. The reality is that social cruelty cannot be carried alone for very long without it having an effect on one's soul. When this happens, there are thousands of spiritual deaths that take place in isolation, having consequences that damage our collective social well-being.

Being spiritually grounded and coming together with others are two important ingredients that are needed in true social reform. This is what has made social movements effective throughout history. It is what made the American civil rights movement so successful, as thousands of people, who experienced or witnessed injustice and cruelty, came together to work in common cause to make our society a better place for all souls, not just some.

The truth is this takes time and dedication. In the process, it is easy to feel like you are surviving in a *Godfather* world while living with an *It's a Wonderful Life* understanding of how things should be. Realities and aspirations are seldom the same, but if we are seeking to build a new and better world for ourselves and our descendants, then we must be able to embody the characteristics of the kind of world we want to live in.

This part of the equation begins with us and starts with our words and worldviews before becoming a part of our outward practices and actions.

It's what Martin Luther King Jr. understood when he said in *Strength to Love*, "Returning hate for hate multiplies hate, adding deeper darkness to a night already devoid of stars. Darkness cannot drive out darkness; only light can do that. Hate cannot drive out hate; only love can do that."[5]

It is why the American civil rights movement was more than Dr. King's charisma and powerful oratory, more than the capable leadership of King, Ralph Abernathy, Rosa Parks, John Lewis, James Farmer, Ella Baker, Andrew Young, Jesse Jackson, and a host of others. It was also successful because of the spiritual disciplines involved in the nonviolent civil disobedience that James Lawson, Myles Horton, and Bayard Rustin taught, the grounding that spiritual guides such as Howard Thurman provided, and the thousands of ordinary people who adopted and applied these spiritual principles to the social and political situations they confronted.

Collectively, they proved that light can drive out darkness and that love can overcome hate. But in order for this to happen, the civil rights leaders and their followers had to gain control of our national narrative, replacing the sameness and uniformity of Lester Maddox with an understanding of the importance of diversity, challenging the injustice of Jim Crow laws with a sense of equity that included everyone, and confronting the exclusionary policies of the George Wallaces of the world with a love centered on inclusion. Eventually, the civil rights agenda became an important part of the American story.

Today, Donald Trump and his followers have seized the national narrative, moved it away from one based on light and love, and replaced it with one characterized by fear, revenge, selfishness, and prejudice. This can most easily be seen in Trump's rendering of "The Snake" story that he frequently used on the campaign trail. The story stands in direct opposition to Jesus' story of the good Samaritan.

5. King, *Strength to Love*, 51.

Trump, the campaigner and candidate for president of the United States, routinely told the story of the snake in his speeches. It represents the spiritual core of his worldview and reveals the essence of Trumpworld.

The good Samaritan story, which Jesus uses in response to a lawyer who was seeking to fulfill the law, be a good neighbor, and lead a worthy life, is based on a message of compassion, a willingness to help out those in need, and the courage to cross cultural lines and prejudices in order to make a positive difference in someone else's life. That's the essence of the good Samaritan worldview and why it has been valued by millions of people over the centuries.

There are even Good Samaritan laws on the books that encourage and provide support for people who render aid to those in need rather than remain bystanders. Countless hospitals are named "Good Samaritan" in honor of the compassion shown in Jesus' story.

Trump's rendering of the story of the snake is based on fear, distrust, and an admonition not to assist others for fear of being taken advantage of or even harmed. In his telling of the encounter, a tenderhearted woman rescues a snake and takes it home only to learn later that the snake is vicious and poisonous. In the story, the snake not only bites the woman and kills her in spite of her generosity, but he also mocks her and calls her silly, indicating that she should have known better than to help him out in the first place. The story puts an exclamation point on Donald Trump's core values and undergirds the philosophy of many of his policy proposals.

These two worldviews take you in antithetical directions and result in completely different ways of being in community with others. No wonder Trumpworld is so willing to tolerate the dismissive, hostile, often cruel behaviors Trump displays.

These qualities are baked into the fundamental understandings of Trumpworld itself, which leads to two sets of rules: one for those like us, and another for others. It is how the mob, cults, and closed societies interpret the world, and it is a part of the narrative that Trump wants us to believe as Americans. It is why he shows up everywhere in American life.

America First and Make America Great Again depend on pronouncements rather than dialogue and conversation. This makes it easy and understandable for someone to remain a by-stander or pass by when someone else is in need by the roadside or when a public policy has negative consequences for an entire group of people.

The goal of authoritarians is to make others feel isolated and discouraged and to become inactive, feeling that the future is in-evitable and beyond their control. In the iconic television show *Star Trek: The Next Generation*, this authoritarian strategy is on full display in the fictional species and feared collective that assimilates others and goes by the name Borg. Representatives of the Borg in-dicate repeatedly to their opponents that "resistance is futile" and that nonresistance and surrender are the only acceptable options available.[6] This is the same approach that dictators utilize against those who oppose them, and total surrender is the goal they seek.

This is why diversity, equity, and inclusion as communal characteristics represent a threat and must be crushed first in Trump's mind. They threaten a two-tiered—us versus them—view of the world upon which everything else hinges. If you are open to a variety of perspectives, purity of thought and simple actions based on a black-and-white worldview become subject to ques-tions, different understandings and conclusions. And that, like the snake in Trump's story, is dangerous.

Instead, it is important to limit contact, narrow perspectives, and "otherize" differences so that control can be maintained. It is the way of authoritarianism and the viewpoint of a despot.

In order for this to be successfully resisted, it will require sig-nificant effort on all our parts. Thankfully, we have both historic guides such as those I've mentioned above as well as current guides such as Maria Ressa (author of *How to Stand Up to a Dictator* and winner of the Nobel Peace Prize), Timothy Synder (author of *On Tyranny*), and many others who are listed in the bibliography and

6. Bole, "Best of Both Worlds."

who have given us helpful guidance on how to deal with despots. We are not alone in the journey. But in order to thrive, we must first learn to be spiritually grounded so we can survive.

If you are holding this book in your hands, chances are you are asking yourself the same kinds of questions that I am asking and that will need to be considered in order to resist the values of Trumpworld and get us to a better place.

The questions we need to be asking are foundational questions, personal identity questions, collective belief questions, like the ones I listed above. They are also questions that demand fundamental, existential, spiritual responses that have to do with the core of who we are as human beings. Such occasions have happened before. We are in such a moment as this now.

In the 1930s, Dietrich Bonhoeffer, the great German pastor, theologian, and anti-Nazi dissident, faced his own version of these questions as he tried to determine not only what he believed most deeply as a person of faith, but also who he wanted to be and what he wanted to do in the context of the rising evil he saw unfolding in his beloved country. Bonhoeffer, who wrote extensively on ethics, Christian discipleship, spiritual life, and the nature of community, ultimately decided to actively resist the rise of Nazism and was imprisoned and executed for his beliefs and actions.

But Bonhoeffer was not alone. Others found their voices, stood up, and paid the price as well. Martin Niemöller, another person of faith, was one of them. While being an early supporter of Hitler, Niemöller eventually saw what was taking place in his country and realized that people, himself included, were being complicit in the evil of the Nazis through their silence.

Eventually, Niemöller found his voice and used it, having been known to have said, "First they came for the Socialists, and I did not speak out, because I was not a Socialist. Then they came for the Trade Unionists, and I did not speak out because I was not a Trade Unionist. Then they came for the Jews, and I did not speak out, because I was not a Jew. Then they came for me, and there was no one left to speak for me."

Couldn't we say something similar today? Perhaps something along these lines: First they came for the immigrants, and I did not speak out, because I was not an immigrant. Then they came for the government workers, and I did not speak out, because I was not a government worker. Then they came for anyone who got in their way, and I did not speak out, because I tried to not get in the way. Then they came for me, and there was no one left to speak for me.

What follows is my attempt to figure out how to live in the growing darkness that is Trumpworld. This means starting by looking at the inner framework that is foundational to this worldview and seeing how it compares to a healthy inner life that is spiritually grounded. How does the past, present, and future function in each of these perspectives? Where do these differing understandings take us as human beings and as a nation?

The chart below, "Charting Your Personal, Spiritual Well-Being," is designed to help you see what spiritual life looks like within each worldview and how developing our spiritual lives will ultimately influence where we end up as a country.

One important part of this is to understand that Trump and Trumpworld have taken the historic and important American values of independence, exploring new frontiers, and self-expression and converted them into the negative qualities of bitterness, hostility, and self-centeredness.

This has thrown off America's ongoing and healthy debate over what should be considered personal and what should be within the public sphere (i.e., individualism versus collectiveness) and has turned it into a messy, contentious struggle that is harming our spiritual lives, sense of national identity, and social well-being.

Charting Your Personal, Spiritual Well-Being

	Past Experiences *Memories, Experiences, Inspirations*	Present Reality *How do you show up in the world?*	Future Orientation *Expectations, Assumptions, Desires*
Trumpworld's Inner Orientation *(an individualistic focus)*	Unresolved hurts and wounds	Trumpworld has converted our sense of independence and personal agency into bitterness, outrage, and anger.	Negative assumptions about new situations
	Grudges and personal slights	Trumpworld has converted the notion of exploring new frontiers into an attitude of hostility and grievance politics.	Revenge
	Stories seen from a first-person narrative point of view only	Trumpworld has taken individualism and self-expression and turned it into self-centeredness, certainty, and purity.	How does this impact me personally? How do things fit into my worldview?

	Past Experiences *Memories, Experiences, Inspirations*	Present Reality *How do you show up in the world?*	Future Orientation *Expectations, Assumptions, Desires*
How Can One Move Toward Inner Health and Spiritual Well-Being? *Cultivating these spiritual qualities will determine whether you move in the direction of Trumpworld or spiritual health.*	**Experience the world with curiosity.** *Don't be afraid of differences in the world or new encounters.*	**Be open to life's new horizons and possibilities.** (Practice the art of "I See You" and asking second questions. Review practices 2 and 12.)	**Diversity** Be open to variety and understand that everyone is unique and different.
	Have a dedicated commitment to compassion *Cruelty is seen as something negative. Refuse to be a bystander and instead intervene as appropriate.*	**Be open to emerging challenges and circumstances** (Find your voice and refuse to be a bystander. Review practices 5, 10, and 11.)	**Equity** Be fair and just. Be aware of inequalities in society.
	Desire community and connection *Living with others is an opportunity to learn. While conflicts are experienced, they don't become walls to connection.*	**Open to others regardless of apparent differences** (Practicing the art of the second question. Review practices 6 and 9.)	**Inclusion** All are welcome. Everyone has value and dignity.

	Past Experiences *Memories, Experiences, Inspirations*	Present Reality *How do you show up in the world?*	Future Orientation *Expectations, Assumptions, Desires*
Healthy Inner Life *(a communal, intercon-nected focus)*	Life and the world are sacred	Wonder and Awe	Being alive and aware in each moment
	Feeling blessed by prior encounters	Gratitude	Open-spirited
	Inclusive narra-tive that consid-ers other voices and perspectives	Communal/ humble/focus on faith	Looking for possibilities and connections

As this chart makes clear, a lot is at stake in terms of the future of our country, depending on where each of us lands in our own spiritual journey. But this journey and the choices we make re-garding it are up to us. *Navigating Trumpworld* is simply an invita-tion to dig a bit deeper into the spiritual realm in order to find our way forward.

A long-standing American conversation has taken place over what we can agree on as being "self-evident" truths (i.e., our common ground) and what latitude we need to create so that each individual is given space to discover and articulate their own un-derstanding of truth.

In other words, what spiritual values need to be central to our understanding of community life? And what expressions, based on culture, conviction, or circumstance, should be given space and voice within the greater whole? This dilemma speaks to why estab-lishing a sense of common ground that allows for diversity, equity, and inclusion to help frame our collective identity is so important, not only to an individual's spiritual journey and sense of dignity but also to the journey of our entire nation.

Parker Palmer put it well when he described the nature of vo-cation in his book *Let Your Life Speak*. Palmer writes, "Before I can tell my life what I want to do with it, I must listen to my life telling me who I am. I must listen for the truths and values at the heart of my own identity, not the standards by which I *must* live."[7] This will not be expressed by all of us in the same manner, but somehow, we must find a way to do this while also moving together in a similar direction.

This collective journey will take time. It will not be a short voyage but a long and ongoing one. In fact, the United States has been on this spiritual journey from the very beginning.

While we have always been a country made up of multiple spiritual frameworks, there are currently two distinct trends that course through our national veins: (1) Trumpworld, with its focus on individualism, grievance, fear, and revenge, and (2) a traditional spirituality grounded in curiosity, wonder, compassion, and kindness. These two divergent approaches explain why our current culture wars center around the concepts of diversity, equity, and inclusion. Our feelings about these three human instincts will ultimately determine the outcome of our current situation.

But the antecedents to our current circumstances go all the way back to the founding of the American experiment. Those precursors should not be overlooked. For example, we're familiar with the fact that the Declaration of Independence was crafted by individuals who believed in the concept "all men are created equal," even as many of them owned slaves. Eventually, this bipolar national identity led to a brutal and costly civil war in which one value system seemed to prevail over the other as the war concluded.

Yet, the charting of America's spiritual values continued to be up for grabs in the midst of Reconstruction, Jim Crow, lynchings and murders, anti-immigrant legislation, internment camps, McCarthyism, the civil rights movement, and the Reagan Revolution, until it finally landed where we find ourselves today with the Trumpworld and the MAGA phenomenon doing battle with old assumptions about the nature of the spiritual life and the values of democracy.

---

7. Palmer, *Let Your Life Speak*, 4–5; emphasis in original.

As we move into this new chapter, whatever happens next will need a great deal of mending. This is where the ancient restorative Japanese art of *kintsugi* comes in.

Kintsugi involves restoring beautiful, but damaged, objects and remaking them into new works of art. This practice serves as a wonderful metaphor for the restorative work ahead of us on both personal and social levels. It is the kind of spiritual work that was involved in the truth and reconciliation commissions in South Africa and Brazil following the trauma of the authoritarian regimes that held power in each of those countries.

As with *kintsugi*, our time must be thoughtfully used and spiritually grounded in order for true restoration to take place and hold the various pieces together. There will be imperfections, flaws, and brokenness present in the final product, but each piece will be a part of an entirely new creation that has renewed value and worth. Part of this work involves understanding that we each contribute to social brokenness in our own way, and part of it involves realizing that we each have something to contribute.

The reality is that all of us can participate in the mending and healing process that is required to restore civility and reclaim our democratic traditions and practices.

The following twelve practices are central to this journey. I hope you will benefit from what I have discovered for myself because we will not accomplish what needs to happen until a large enough number of us step back to reflect on what is occurring today and decide that the foundational questions and the practices I am recommending in the following pages can be utilized to help shape a new direction based on compassion, kindness, honesty, justice, and social reflection.

This is ultimately a humble task worthy of everyone who is a part of a democratic society. As Americans, we are first and foremost fellow human beings—nothing more, nothing less. It is a reality of life that unites us with the rest of the world, regardless of race, culture, or national origin. And contrary to our self-image of being unique and exceptional in relationship to others, like everyone else, we have our virtues and vices, our positives and negatives, our unique insights and our collective blind spots, our demons and our better angels. This is something that Sinclair Lewis was keenly aware of when he wrote *It Can't Happen Here*, because the reality is that it can.

The "chosen people" syndrome that has arisen at different points in history from the ancient Hebrews and Romans to America's current version of being better than everyone else in the world is the kind of arrogance that ultimately spawns hatred toward others, colonialism, and aggression. This notion is central to Trumpworld's view of things, but it is a small step to take from righteousness to self-righteousness. When this happens there is a separation that naturally occurs between people, creating an us versus them, good versus bad, right versus wrong mindset. It is a recipe for despotism, and it is what happens when a people lose their capacity to be self-reflective.

There is not a lot of room for diverse voices and unique perspectives in an authoritarian universe. In fact, when any nation or group of people become "the chosen," in spiritual terms, it serves as a form of idolatry, making a specific group of people "better than" everyone else. In the process, that group replaces their god, in whatever form that might be, with themselves.

The current American version of this worldview is especially troubling because so much power and privilege undergirds its present manifestation. This brand of self-righteousness and exceptionalism must stop. It is not only dangerous, but it is the currency of bullies, braggarts, and tyrants. Unfortunately, it is currently being applied with great effect within the realm of Trumpworld.

What this means is that now is the time to wake up and be alert. Pay attention. Ground ourselves. Return to spiritually oriented ways. It is time to come together as people who are concerned about our collective future and determine how best to live out our values in harmony with others. Howard Thurman, in his book *The Search for Common Ground*, opened the book by asking the question, "How can I be me without making it difficult for you to be you?"[8] This is a challenging proposition, but it is a question we must start asking ourselves on a regular basis.

Fortunately, there is still a window of time in which to change our national trajectory, but that window of opportunity is rapidly closing. I fear for what will happen once it shuts.

What we do next will be critical to the outcome, and it will require a spiritual understanding of the world. It will involve a movement from personal to social growth, and it will require discipline. Richard Foster put it well in his classic work *Celebration of Discipline*: "Superficiality is the curse of our age. The doctrine of instant satisfaction is a primary spiritual problem. The desperate need today is not for a greater number of intelligent people, or gifted people, but for deep people."[9]

I remember as a young boy reading presidential candidate George McGovern's political pamphlet in 1972 in which he asked voters the question, "What kind of people are we?" It was a deeply spiritual challenge coming from a person running for president of the United States. It may have been too deep of a question for people to respond to if they didn't want to be bothered with such things. But the truth is that we cannot become the kind of nation we want to be until each of us takes up this question on a personal basis.

I hope that the twelve practices that follow can help us become deeper people together. In the process, we may learn how to regain our collective footing, reclaim our spirits, preserve our hope, and discover our resilience.

Until we are centered, rooted, and grounded in values and practices that are more substantial and compassionate than those emanating from Trumpworld, we can't hope to withstand the vicissitudes of the present moment nor the chaos, confusion, and cruelty that are a part of the world we are creating.

8. Thurman, *Search for Common Ground*, xi.
9. Foster, *Celebration of Discipline*, 1.

Practice 1

Live Life Inside Out

LIFE MOVES IN AN inward-out manner—from thought to action, from policy to practice, from intention to consequence. Spiritual guides throughout the centuries have reminded us of this reality in one way or another.

It is why so many philosophers have focused their attention on the notion of the human soul or inner spirit, often referring to them as our window into the world. It is this inner space—what one might call our essential being or humanity—that determines what we see, how we see, and what we value as we engage ourselves with our surroundings.

A healthy inner life looks out into the world with curiosity and a desire to learn and grow from what we see and experience. This perspective is at the heart of Mónica Guzman's book *I Never Thought of It That Way* and why she guided her readers in "how to have fearlessly curious conversations in dangerously divided times." This is important because when things aren't well with our inner lives, the world becomes distorted and resembles a place filled with fear, hostility, and negativity, and we lose our curiosity and interest in learning.

As we consider what is taking place within the United States today, it is fundamentally important to remember to care for one's inner life and well-being lest we lose track of the beliefs and spiritual grounding that are essential to meaning-making and that ultimately give substance and value to our actions.

Spirituality is organic in nature, which makes it harder to understand. Doctrine is more rigid and makes it easy to create paradigms such as us and them, right or wrong, good and bad. Faith is about wonder, curiosity, humility, uncertainty, even doubt. Doctrine and law focus our attention much more on uniformity and certainty. One depends on creating a learning community; the other, on people willing to follow rules and orders.

In 2020, when I wrote my book *Rediscovering the Spirit: From Political Brokenness to Spiritual Wholeness* at the conclusion of the Trump 1.0 administration, I listed four qualities that I believe are essential to achieving spiritual wholeness: centering, framing, practicing, and living with others. These four qualities, as they engage, influence, and interact with each other, shape both the kind of human beings we become and the kind of world we create.

They also reflect the reality that there is a natural interplay and constant movement that takes place between our inner lives and our social settings. This interplay occurs in an inside-out manner.

It is why I agree with these words, which are often attributed to Lao Tzu, the sixth-century BC Chinese philosopher:

> If there is to be peace in the nations, there must be peace in the cities.
>
> If there is to be peace in the cities, there must be peace between neighbors.
>
> If there is to be peace between neighbors, there must be peace in the home.
>
> If there is to be peace in the home, there must be peace in the heart.[1]

The state of our world is determined by the struggles that first take place within our own spirits and between the muses and the demons that reside there. Our inner life is where our various voices

1. Author unknown, though it is often credited to Lao Tzu in the Tao Te Ching. It most closely relates to entry 54. See Le Guin, *Lao Tzu*, 79.

and perspectives are first heard and given the freedom to speak, where our inspiration to act resides, and where our words are first formed before they are spoken aloud.

Given the many ways in which Trumpworld attempts to violate the basic spiritual understandings of life, diminish their value, and replace them with an objectification of people and a transactional approach to human interaction, it is vitally important to remember that we are all spiritual beings and that the world is a sacred place. Once we understand this, it is easy to see ourselves being a part of something much greater than ourselves and realize that we are interrelated with and depend on each other.

This is not to say that Trumpworld does not care about inner values. It does. All worldviews have values embedded within them. The problem we are facing today is that the values of Trumpworld undermine the essential teachings that undergird most spiritual traditions, replacing them with actions grounded in prejudice, vengefulness, closed-mindedness, and hatred. When these characteristics dominate how one functions in the world, we have a spiritual problem that must be addressed at a deep level that goes well beyond politics.

When we practice the spiritual disciplines of humility, awe, curiosity, and wonder, we naturally begin to move along a spiritual path. It is why it is so important to not let Trumpworld's values and understandings of people and creation take hold of us. This would be like taking a hike in the wilderness without having a compass or markers to guide us on our way.

In order to confront Trumpworld, our engagement with the greater cosmos must be from inward out, but only after we have taken the time needed to respond rather than simply react to what is occurring around us. This means beginning by uncovering our best selves and making those qualities central to our actions. This takes time and a willingness to be self-reflective.

But this is a difficult challenge living in a fast-paced setting and under the conditions of Trumpworld, which has little patience for self-reflection and social encounters with those who come from different cultures, perspectives, or races, and dismisses spiritual concerns as weak and antithetical to material wealth and blind loyalty.

For me, this leads to an important maxim and related corollary that influences how we should function in the world: What is personal is sacred, and what is public is for all. Likewise, everything is sacred, and everyone is connected. Because of this, authoritarian regimes always try to privatize public things and publicize private things.

This is done in order to both expand control over public life and increase a sense of fear among the resistance and opposition. But sacredness and spirituality operate in a different way by both honoring what is held in common and recognizing the value of those things that are personal in nature.

The American Buddhist teacher Pema Chodron put it well when she said, "*Bodhichitta* is a Sanskrit word that means 'noble or awakened heart.' It is said to be present in all beings. Just as butter is inherent in milk and oil is inherent in a sesame seed, this soft spot is inherent in you and me. . . . No matter how committed we are to unkindness, selfishness, or greed, the genuine heart of *bodhichitta* cannot be lost."[2] What this means is that we must become aware of our own awakened heart and realize that it is present in everyone and everything else as well.

We are all a part of the same creation, and what affects one part ultimately affects the whole. This means that the interplay between our inner well-being and our social reality needs to be honored. This must be done in an inside out manner so that a healthy spirituality can emerge in the world, allowing darkness to be consumed by light and negativity to be diminished by thoughtful goodness and mutual consideration.

Indigenous cultures and tribal societies have long understood such things since the community is a highly valued part of these worldviews. But the ability to do this is a shortcoming within our more individualistic, capitalist understanding of things. As a result, it is easy in our society for aggression, anger, and selfishness to consume us and negatively impact those around us, creating

2. Chodron, *Pocket Pema Chodron*, 1–2.

division and brokenness. Trumpworld has taken advantage of this human tendency, and the result is the creation of a kind of "grievance politics" that wants to get even with the rest of the world and blame others for any perceived slights or limitations.

We have much to learn from those cultures that see the world in more collectivist terms. It is why democracy matters so much to a Western civilization understanding of the world and why things like climate change, international alliances and treaties, and the Declaration of Human Rights matter in the larger scheme of things. They are reminders that we are all connected, but that connection begins in the human heart.

When we are standing on common ground, life often opens up, and we find ourselves standing on sacred ground as well. This doesn't require much of us other than being open to something or someone new, a willingness to be curious and learn, and the humility to return to basics.

Because Trumpworld is fundamentally an outward-in movement of the spirit rather than an inward-out movement, it has a tendency to get stuck and become obsessed with externals. This results in those under its spell expressing a politics of grievance and being preoccupied with blaming others, seeking revenge, and getting even. In such a world, it is difficult to find the foundational spiritual qualities of compassion, grace, and forgiveness being alive and well. They simply don't fit the worldview of us versus them, friends and enemies, those who are right and everyone else.

When we create a truly spiritually grounded framework for ourselves, no one should feel as if they are an object or widget in Trumpworld's grand scheme for domination and order. An "America first" attitude negates the inward-out movement by seeing the world in terms of us and them, in which some are pure and others are less than.

An inward-out lifestyle creates space for each person to be valued as a human being—unique and special, a work in progress. This is a critical first step in overcoming Trumpworld's degradation of the human spirit. It is something that we need to recognize in ourselves and honor when we meet others. We may not all agree, but we do share a common humanity and carry a spark of the divine within us.

How different Donald Trump might become if we asked him some essential questions to help ground him in spiritual reality, such as these: Who are your spiritual guides? What values orient your life? What relationships shape your sense of community? What did you learn from your parents? What is it like to be a husband and father? What are your hopes for your family? What are your personal regrets and shortcomings?

In recent years, Donald Trump has led a powerful political revolution that has had a profound, negative spiritual impact on the United States. Barring a significant economic downturn or an international crisis, the only antidote for this will be the arrival of a spiritual revolution that challenges Trumpworld and moves our politics in a positive direction.

Trumpworld will not change until the conversation changes, becomes more human, and we begin to dialogue about basic values rather than public policies first. It is the inward-out way of living in the world.

Practice 2

Be Fully Awake
and Let Others Know You See Them

SUSAN AND I HAVE delivered for Meals on Wheels every week to seniors in our area since the fall of 2019. Not long ago, we attended the congregate meal that is served to those who come into the senior center to eat. It was our first time participating in this meal. When we entered the space, we looked around the room and sat down at a table with a couple who were sitting alone.

We had never met them before, so we introduced ourselves and discovered that the couple were Chinese immigrants who had moved to the United States to live with their daughter three years ago. We quickly learned that they did not speak English. We do not speak Mandarin. Given our language barrier, this situation could have easily become uncomfortable for all of us.

But this is not what happened. Instead, Susan immediately pulled out her phone and started using Google Translate as a way to overcome this barrier and introduce ourselves to our tablemates. Through this process, we learned about their family, which quickly led us into a conversation about something we shared in common—grandchildren. And before long, we were exchanging photos and exploring the various dimensions of our many human connections through the wonder of Google Translate.

On one level, it wasn't a very complicated conversation, but it was a deeply human one. It began by us first seeing each other, then sharing some basic information about our families and, as a result, connecting with each other through our life stories. By the end of the conversation, we had stepped toward each other rather than let a difference—even a difference in language—become a barrier that defined our time together. It wasn't an earth-shattering experience, but it reflects how relationships are created and how community can be formed through simple encounters with each other.

A couple days later, a friend of mine, Kristinoel, emailed a personal experience that she had while waiting for a friend at the hospital. She shared her story with a writers' group that we both belong to.

In her story, Kristinoel described how she happened to encounter one of the hospital custodians, who was taking care of the plants, and asked her a question. After she did that, the custodian came close, and together they fiddled with some moss in one of the big potted plants in the lobby.

After a short time, the custodian spread her arms wide, smiled big, and said that talking with my friend *es como un rayito del sol*—was a ray of sunshine! My friend said that she felt her warmth in return.

As it turns out, this custodian was from Oaxaca, Mexico, and when Kristinoel asked her if she interacted with people as she worked, the custodian replied, "No, maybe to them I am invisible, part of the hospital scene, like the large potted plants."

Kristinoel closed her email saying, "I am reminded how each day we are given simple invitations to share our humanity."[1]

Like Susan and my encounter with the Chinese couple at the senior center, this wasn't a very difficult thing for Kristinoel to do, but it made a world of difference to those involved and for an instant deepened our sense of human community with each other.

Isn't it ironic that at a time when there are more people in the world than ever before, we often find ourselves struggling with the

---

1. Kristinoel, email message, Apr. 21, 2025.

basic principles of how to deepen our sense of human connection with each other?

One of the fundamental practices of most spiritual traditions involves practicing the art of being fully awake and aware of life around us. It is an essential part of being alive.

In the Christian Gospels, Jesus tells his disciples to stay awake and be alert on numerous occasions, even lamenting the fact that they aren't able to stay awake while he is being arrested and betrayed. At one point, Jesus says, "Why are you sleeping? Get up and pray so that you will not fall into temptation" (Luke 22:46).

Being awake is about readiness, vigilance, and alertness. It has to do with watching for the ways in which God is at work in the world. In Buddhism, wakefulness is about being mindful and alert, which are essential ingredients to being fully present.

In a way, the whole of spiritual life depends on being "woke"—not in the sense of reaching an endpoint or destination in one's journey, but in terms of being open to the surrounding world and those who inhabit it. In Trumpworld, however, this characteristic is often demeaned and criticized. Yet, being awake (i.e., woke) has to do with living life fully, being aware, alert, attentive, and observant.

These are the qualities that help keep one humble in light of the complexity of the world and the diversity that is central to it. Being in love with the world and with others is about paying attention to everything around us in all its wonderful diversity, by going outside ourselves and actually seeing others.

This way of being has to do with how we encounter those we meet along the way. Perhaps we'd do well to consider the African Zulu greeting *Sawubona*, which means "I see you." In order to truly see others, we need to be awake, not asleep, to the world—interested, not judgmental or dismissive.

In this African tradition, when a person says *Sawubona*, the appropriate response is *Ngikhona*, which means "I am here," or sometimes translated, "It is good to be seen." We cannot truly see each other as fellow human beings if we are not first paying attention.

This simple exchange in greeting communicates dignity and a willingness to acknowledge someone else's presence in the world. To be noticed by others is to have one's significance recognized, which is something we all appreciate. Greeting one another by seeing each other is the first step in human connection, even between strangers and passersby, because the truth is we do not know the struggles and burdens another person is carrying, and to have someone simply say "I see you" adds a sense of respect to life and builds a sense of community.

In their training video on empathy and compassion, the Cleveland Clinic reminds us about how important it is to be awake and pay attention to others. The video simply takes viewers through a hospital, meeting various patients and medical personnel along the way, and, without using spoken words, shows us what various people are experiencing in their lives. They are things that you might not know about a person you pass by, even if you are paying close attention.

As the video demonstrates, it could be that the person we encounter just heard that their cancer is in remission or that it has metastasized. It may be that someone is seeing a family member for the last time or that someone hasn't had a day off in seven days. It could be that someone just learned that they are going to be a father for the first time or that they won't be able to make a family wedding because of an illness. Oftentimes, we simply don't know what is going on with someone else when we encounter them on our daily round.

Then the video ends with these words being flashed across a series of screens: "If you could stand in someone else's shoes, hear what they hear, see what they see, feel what they feel, would you treat them differently?" These words are a helpful reminder that greeting another person in a way that says "I see you," while being a simple gesture, is first and foremost an act of love.[2]

At the same time, in *I'm Still Here*, the Brazilian movie that won the 2024 Oscar for Best International Feature Film, Eunice Paiva refuses to go away even after the 1970 military dictatorship

2. Cleveland Clinic, "Empathy."

kidnaps, tortures, and kills her husband, abducts her and her daughter for questioning, and intimidates Eunice with constant surveillance. Eunice remains undaunted and goes on to get her law degree, press for information about the whereabouts of her husband, and eventually becomes an outspoken representative of indigenous rights in the Amazon.[3] Eunice is an amazing example of what a well-grounded, courageous human being can do with their life by remaining present and showing up day after day.

Seeing others in everyday life and refusing to go unseen by those in authority are both critical elements of opposing fascism and authoritarianism. These are the essential human qualities that replace blindness with seeing, silence with using one's voice, and closed-mindedness with an open spirit.

This is what is so troubling about the Trump administration's current efforts to eliminate, even whitewash, the rich history of our nation's diverse voices. This endeavor has not only included the firing of anyone associated with diversity, equity, and inclusion programs but also the attempt to remove the names of some twenty-six thousand individuals from our military records and other public acknowledgments.[4]

Some of these efforts have included removing the names of historical heroes such as Jackie Robinson, members of the Tuskegee Airmen, and others who don't fit a narrow, ideological narrative of American greatness. How can we gain a full picture of our nation's history if those in power single-handedly decide whose story can be included and whose story must be purged from our national narrative? When we reduce our understanding of the bravery, creativity, and endurance of others, we simultaneously reduce our own capacity to develop courage, insight, and resilience in our lives.

It seems only fair to ask those with this kind of authority, "What is the criteria being used to exclude Americans from US history?" And therefore, on what basis are people being included and how do these qualities relate to America's ideals? Being seen

3. Salles, *I'm Still Here.*
4. Associated Press, "War Heroes."

matters. It determines how our collective story is told and how history is written.

One of the fundamental dangers of Trumpworld's understanding of community has to do with the fact that when you see the world operating in an "us versus them" framework, it is easy to objectify, commodify, and demean others, especially those you choose to demonize. While this characteristic is not unique to Trumpworld, whenever this happens within the human community, both the human spirit and life itself are diminished.

The notions of "I see you" and "I'm still here" are connected. If I don't see you, I can't understand you, I can't value you as a fellow human being, and I am unable to give you the dignity you deserve. Being able to say "I'm still here" means that nothing you do can take away my right to exist and be valued, my right to have a voice, my right to live. We all have agency in the world, and no one has a right to take that away maliciously!

Without everyone being valued, it makes it difficult to create a stable, civil society.

Within the confines of Trumpworld, much has been made about the idea of being "woke." It has become a lightning rod for Trumpworld adherents, as if it represents a form of evil within the framework of that universe. In fact, in Donald Trump's March 2025 address to Congress, he proclaimed, "Our country will be woke no longer."[5] For a Trump follower, this translates into the notion that being awake is something bad in itself, even though most spiritual guides, including Jesus himself, say that being awake is the ultimate goal of being fully alive and spiritually whole.

Who doesn't want to be awake to life in all its richness? Isn't this how we come to understand and know one another? Wakefulness is how we pay attention and notice our surroundings. Wakefulness is the opposite of being asleep and disinterested.

Perhaps the reality is that Trumpworld's survival depends on people being asleep, disinterested, and unaware. When this happens, we don't pay attention to each other or to what is really going on around us, and when this happens, things take place without

5. Grabenstein, "Trump Says."

being fully comprehended. Evil and ill intent often lurk in such places. That's why wakefulness is the first step in confronting injustice and resisting evil.

Practice 3

Stay Informed but Not Obsessed

WHILE IT IS CRITICAL to be open-spirited, well-informed, and aware of one's surroundings, it is also crucial not to allow what is sacred, precious, and central to one's humanity be demeaned, diminished, or smudged by the negativity that surrounds us every day. It is all too easy, especially in our current twenty-four seven social media world, to let outside news and realities invade the recesses of our inner life, leaving us discouraged, despairing, and depressed.

This can easily happen because what is deeply valued is constantly being challenged. This happens when things that are not factual are portrayed as being true. And the volume of information coming at us on a daily basis can be overwhelming. There's just a lot to sort out—constantly.

While it is important to honor the natural dance that occurs between our spiritual lives and the events that are a part of our social settings, we must not allow ourselves to be consumed by those external activities to the point of obsession, especially when they reflect hatreds, prejudices, hostility toward others, and detrimental falsehoods.

Trumpworld feeds and thrives on the chaos that this constant barrage of information has on our lives, hoping we'll be drawn into external fights while leaving our spiritual centers unprotected. Information without thoughtful reflection can become addictive and destructive. When this happens, simply take a step back and reflect on what is occurring. When we immerse ourselves too much in the news of the world, our spiritual lives can be altered dramatically.

Put in contemporary, popular cultural terms, it is essentially what Yoda teaches Luke Skywalker about the power of the dark side in the *Star Wars* movies, observing that it is anger, fear, and aggression that represent the dark side because those are the inner forces that can capture your attention and lead you astray. Yoda's guidance to Luke is that once you start down that path, the dark side can dominate your life and control your future.

In other words, being obsessed by the negative leads to being spiritually imbalanced at the core of one's being. This makes it hard to respond to challenging external matters in a wholistic and value-centered manner. Trumpworld seeks to bring about this kind of inner imbalance.

At some point, one must be like Dorothy in *The Wizard of Oz* or Joseph Welch during the 1954 Army-McCarthy hearings and gather up the relevant evidence one is facing and speak truth to power in a measured, grounded, and clear manner.

In the case of *The Wizard of Oz*, it is Dorothy who in her quest to return home to the safety of Kansas finds the inner courage she needs in order to confront the apparent all-powerful Wizard of Oz. In response to her defiance, the wizard presents Dorothy with the challenge of having to do battle with the Wicked Witch of the West and bring back her broom as evidence of her success.

Later, it is Toto, Dorothy's dog, who overpowers the Wizard of Oz's public persona by pulling back the curtain and revealing the truth about who he really is. Once exposed as a fraud, the wizard loses his hold on those who fear him.

Dorothy and her friends, having gained strength from each other as they overcome challenge after challenge throughout their journey, demonstrate that their collective voice can make a difference and that since the wizard has used his power to frighten people and harm others rather than do good, he isn't really great at all. Instead, he is a pathetic old man who needs to be questioned and held accountable for his actions. But this happens because

Dorothy and her friends become informed by the realities they must confront, yet are not overwhelmed by them.

In real life, on June 9, 1954, in the Army-McCarthy hearings, it was the attorney Joseph Welch who finally helped turn the tide against Senator McCarthy's cruelty when he said, "Have you no sense of decency, sir, at long last?" Welch pulled back the curtain as well when he went on to say what many Americans already felt in their hearts, based on what they had seen for themselves but were afraid to say: "Until this moment, Senator, I think I never really gauged your cruelty, or your recklessness."[1]

Welch believed that McCarthy was actually trying to assassinate the character and essence of America by his actions. And like Dorothy, Welch was courageous enough to speak truth to power, and it made a difference. Both he and Dorothy were well-informed by the facts and their personal experience. At the same time, they both remained grounded and spiritually centered when challenged by abusive power.

Sometimes the news of the day can become overwhelming and be too much. My wife, Susan, has a good way of turning a dinner conversation around when it has gotten too full of Trump-world matters and has become overly consuming. She simply says, "I didn't invite Donald Trump to have dinner with us tonight." This comment helpfully redirects the conversation, saying, "That's enough negativity for now. Let's enjoy our time together."

Yes, it is important to follow the news, listen to people's real-life stories about what is happening as a result of Trumpworld's assumptions and the Trump administration's policy decisions, and then decide how best to proceed based on what you have learned. But in order to respond to the constant barrage of negative challenges effectively, it is critical to remain spiritually grounded and behave from a place of spiritual strength. This is difficult to do when you feel overwhelmed, which is a good reminder of the helpful advice that Michelle Obama gave us back in 2016: "When they

1. American Experience, "Have You No Decency?," 3:42; United States Senate, "Have You No Sense."

go low, we go high."[2] From a spiritual perspective, it could also be said, when they go shallow, we go deep.

2. Bruner, "Michelle Obama Explains."

Practice 4

Understand That Emotions Are Contagious

RICHARD ROHR, THE FRANCISCAN priest and author, writes, "If we do not transform our pain, we will most assuredly transmit it."[1] There is a lot of pain floating about in the world these days, and much of it is transmitted to others as a result of not being transformed before it is shared.

People experience abuses of one kind or another all the time. Folks have their hopes and dreams dashed before they can be realized. A number of individuals are recipients of prejudice or experience the direct effects of racism simply based on the color of their skin, the culture they are a part of, or their personal sense of identity. Sometimes feelings of being a part of a "we" suddenly turn into the experience of being one of "them." Whatever form it takes, such dehumanizing experiences, and the dismissals and diminishments that accompany them, cause both pain and anger.

Anyone who has ever been a part of someone else's debriefing of a negative experience in which they felt attacked, angered, violated, or diminished knows that such feelings can easily be passed on to you while someone else is sharing what they are feeling. This happens because it is nearly impossible to keep pain to one's self without it leaking out in some fashion. This leaking out is passed

1. Rohr, "Transforming Pain."

61

from one person to another until it can be transformed in some way. Not until then can the damage taking place be ameliorated.

I remember once when one of our daughters called me on her way home from work saying, "I've had a bad day." She went on to express in vivid and emotional terms how angry she was about what had happened when someone at work got mad at her. I listened and absorbed what she said and soon became upset myself.

When my wife, Susan, got home from work, I began describing to her what our daughter experienced and could feel myself getting worked up in the retelling of her story. As a result, Susan became upset about what had happened as well. The transmission of the initial anger was passed on.

In this situation, one person's anger had been transferred to someone else, and then that secondary anger got passed on yet again as if it was contagious. Anger, like pain, if not transformed, is transmitted. This is true for most emotions, good and bad, positive and negative. Emotions can be contagious.

I sense the volatility of this more today than ever as people become upset about one news story or another, one policy decision or another. The danger is that when nothing is transformed, everything is transmitted. This does not make for a healthy society.

In the worst cases, a violent act is involved and transmitted to the lives of others, many of whom are completely innocent and not even associated with what caused the anger or frustration in the first place. Once there, these toxins continue to have an effect on everyone's life, even years later.

I think about the recent thirtieth anniversary of the Oklahoma City bombing of the federal building on April 19, 1995. Whatever else was going on in the lives of Timothy McVeigh and Terry Nichols in the days leading up to that fateful event, one thing is clear: they did not overcome nor transform the emotions of hatred they felt toward the federal government at that time, and they became obsessed and consumed by their inner demons. As a result, these two individuals proceeded to bomb the Alfred P. Murrah Federal Building, taking the lives of 168 people and injuring an additional 684 individuals, many of them children.

Their inability to avoid being consumed by hatred, negative emotions, and the dehumanization of others was a deadly mix and meant that McVeigh and Nichols's actions, while being based on the hostility they obviously held, also were reactive in nature. Somehow what was going on in their lives allowed them to avoid self-reflection, spiritual grounding, and communal connection with others. The deep, spiritual values that frame and define a democratic society weren't even part of the equation for them.

One of the defining traits of Trumpworld is to create a reactive environment in which things are said or done that charge emotions—often dealing with feelings of resentment or revenge—circumvent normal spiritual, values-based processing, and result in reactive responses that undercut self-reflection and escalate the energy in the air.

Donald Trump is a master at this and has the ability to agitate, blame others, and keep things stirred up emotionally. And the truth is, this can create an adrenaline rush and even become addictive for some people. When this process gets initiated, a well-grounded, spiritual response is what is needed in order to short-circuit this negative, hostile chain of events and replace it with curiosity, conversation, and connection.

In the aftermath of the federal building tragedy in 1995, many Oklahoma City citizens were able to rise up from the devastation and pain of that moment and through kindness, service, and resilience create what became known as "the Oklahoma Standard."

Remarkably, countless people in that wounded community went deep within their spirits, discovered their "better angels," and were somehow able to work through their pain and grief, come out the other side, and find a path forward that brought healing and civic contributions to others rather than let anger or revenge consume them and allow the presence of these toxins and contagions to persist in their lives. All of us have much to learn from those who transformed their pain into something positive to become a living legacy of their love for those who lost their lives on that day.

In our current situation, with all the aggressive and harsh political talk and policy decisions, it becomes much more challenging because you often have no clear or immediate recourse to random acts of unkindness and injustice. Something happens to you as a result of someone else's decision and suddenly your freedom is taken away or you lose your job or you're publicly demeaned, and there is nothing you can immediately do about it. Sometimes it is difficult to transform something so random and hurtful into something constructive when others have power and you appear to have none.

I saw this phenomenon at play recently when I attended several public town halls and witnessed people's pain and anger on full display. Many of those present were clearly upset and didn't know what their recourse was other than to express (i.e., transmit) their pain and anger to their elected representatives, hoping that they would be heard and that something could be done. It was difficult for these elected officials, who themselves felt helpless, to say much more than "I feel your pain." It was a helpful first step, but not the stuff of transformation.

Making a real difference in these situations is easier said than done. To begin with, democratic politics isn't clear-cut or immediate, and second, those in Trumpworld are either incredibly tone deaf or simply aren't interested in the pain others are experiencing or concerned with collective transformation.

Yet, in order for the damage to become a scar rather than an open wound, slowly but surely transformation in some form has to take place or the damage will become permanent—and will eventually be passed on to others.

So, what does one do to stop the bleeding and prevent the further transmission of negative emotions?

Of course, this depends on the nature of the wound and the degree of pain being experienced. For some, what has taken place is life altering: the loss of a job; agency over your own body being denied; the public release of private, personal information that results in harmful damage being done; deportation.

For others, it is more akin to what the fictional character Howard Beale says in the movie *Network*: "I'm as mad as hell, and I'm not going to take this anymore."[2]

One's response to what is taking place today may require different actions depending on what has actually happened. These reactions could include everything from lawsuits to organizing and protesting with others, to more personal things such as journaling or therapy. In the days ahead, there will be elections to vote in, volunteering to be done, and petitions to sign. Whatever the response is, however, in the end it must contribute to the movement toward a more meaningful and transformative world. Otherwise, it will fester and damage one's own soul and maintain a level of social dysfunction without improving connections and deepening a sense of community.

This is why it is crucial to have healthy ways in which to transform and release the negative energy one has experienced. And this may well mean not expecting a positive outcome within Trumpworld since these kinds of pain and personal harm are not respected or valued by those in positions of power. It is not the primary currency of that world, and those with power often do not care about the human costs of those being harmed. Within an emerging dictatorship, this will become even more likely.

Personally, I'm more in the "mad as hell" camp at the present time since, for the most part, I've avoided direct, personal harm. As a result, for me, practicing the principles outlined in this book and actually writing these pages has been part of my transformation process. I simply grew tired of randomly expressing and transmitting the pain I was experiencing to others as I grieved the loss of my country. Yes, I have participated in protest rallies, written cards to encourage people in other states to vote, and attended the town halls of my representatives as well, which is also part of my healing and resistance.

This may seem to be an inadequate response to a growing national danger, but to transmit rather than transform one's anger and pain simply adds fuel to the fire and gives more power to those

2. Lumet, *Network*.

who have caused the pain in the first place. I don't want to aid and abet their efforts in any way. The atmosphere of an entire nation is at stake, so negative energy only adds to our collective problem. However, each of us can take small, meaningful steps that hopefully make a difference in the larger scheme of things.

In this case, it is good to remember what the freedom riders experienced during the civil rights movement of the 1950s and 1960s and what John Lewis taught us in his book *Walking with the Wind*. Lewis focused his attention on living a nonviolent life, even as he went about making "good trouble." Lewis focused on love, saying,

> The sense of love realizes that emotions of the moment and constantly shifting circumstances can cloud that divine spark. Pain, ugliness, and fear can cover it over, turning a person toward anger and hate. It is the ability to see through those layers of ugliness, to see further into a person than perhaps that person can see into himself, that is essential to the practice of nonviolence.[3]

I have experienced my own forms of pain but nothing like what John Lewis experienced throughout his life. If John Lewis could face what he faced and transform it through love and his commitment to nonviolence, then I want to be a part of that movement, because that's what will lead to real transformation.

---

3. Lewis, *Walking with the Wind*, 77.

Practice 5

Discover Your Voice and Share Stories

Sharing stories is how we make a home within ourselves and one another. Story is how we put together the broken pieces. Story is how we identify and heal the suffering within and among us. The practice of storytelling, particularly when sharing the real stories from our own living, tethers us to what matters most—our families, our friends, nature, the hearts we carry, the wondrous mystery of life itself. Every human being longs for a good question and a listening ear.

—Mark Yaconelli

OUR LANGUAGE, WORDS, AND stories help define who we are as individuals and as a society. When we exchange stories with each other, we not only share experiences, but we build trust, understand each other better, and form community.

The basic problem with Trumpworld is that it demands uniformity, depends on total allegiance, values one voice, and has a single-minded view of the world. Everyone is supposed to conform to its ideas and demands, and those ideas center around one person.

But creation isn't designed in this way, and people—especially Americans—have a deep urge to be free. There are millions of species in the world, countless cultures and belief systems, and an array of ways in which to perceive and live in the world. America is filled with diversity. No wonder the emerging principles of diversity, inclusion, and equity are fundamentally American. They help us to both heal past wounds and stretch our social canvas at the same time.

But for Trumpworld, its uni-vision approach to public policy and human interactions means that those who don't fit neatly into Trumpworld's prevailing worldview will ultimately be ostracized, exiled, or punished in some form until we comply. It is a purity of race approach to living, which means that for most of us we simply won't fit, won't measure up, and won't be free to live our lives without the fear of disapproval or reprisal. This is on one level a narrow, constrictive way of seeing the world. At its worst, it is downright abusive.

In Trumpworld, it is just a matter of time before everyone will be forced to comply with the sense of order being laid out in a Project 2025 understanding of how the world should be. There will be those in charge and then the rest of us. It is a disturbing prospect because independence and finding one's voice and using it for the collective good is the basis upon which strong communities are formed.

The use of public language is a key part of things. The language of love is the basis upon which community is built. Hatred causes alienation and division. Stories of inclusion expand how community is experienced by others. Uniformity shrinks the world and forces some into exile or marginalization. Words of affirmation keep hopes and dreams alive. Revenge and accusation damage the human spirit. These polarities lead to the creation of completely different societies, and today these polarities are actively competing for our attention. One approach leads naturally toward democracy, the other toward authoritarianism.

This is where telling stories and listening to the stories of others comes in. As Mark Yaconelli says, telling stories can be a healing experience and help us overcome brokenness. Stories provide the mortar of a healthy community foundation. But this doesn't happen by accident. It must be intentional.

I think about this in terms of Michele Norris's long-standing Race Card Project. Simply put, Norris was able to uncover thousands of stories from people—well over five hundred thousand, to be more exact—by asking individuals to send her their six-word responses to this prompt: "Race. Your Story. Six Words. Please Send."[1] She documents the breadth and complexity of these simple, six-word responses in her remarkable book *Our Hidden Conversations: What Americans Really Think About Race and Identity.*

In the fourteen years since Norris first posed this question, she has heard all kinds of stories. They have been shocking, painful, triumphant, angry, and often filled with exhaustion, candor, bigotry, and regret. It seems like people have a lot to say in this country about their experience with race. And unless and until we deal with the complexity of these stories, we will not heal or overcome the racism that has plagued us for centuries. Sharing our stories can help us reach that goal and become a better people in the process.

The great Brazilian educator Paulo Freire taught this principle by simply showing people pictures of their communities and asking them if and where they saw themselves in the image. It was the kind of visual prompt that helped people gain a sense of personal identity and begin to tell their story to others. But in order for stories to gain value, there must be willing and interested listeners. And that's where we all come in.

Within a democracy, this means that those with power must be willing to listen to ordinary people so that everyone's voice can be heard and valued as decisions are being made. This means holding town halls and public hearings, making oneself available, and taking time to listen as well as talk. A good rule of thumb is that those who aren't willing to listen don't make good leaders because they aren't willing to listen to the viewpoints of a variety of people as they form their opinions and policies.

1. Norris, *Our Hidden Conversations*, xvi.

Think about it in terms of what happened when Nelson Mandela was elected president of South Africa in 1994. The Truth and Reconciliation Commission that Desmond Tutu headed was formed almost immediately in 1995, giving people the opportunity to tell their stories publicly. Those who had been harmed by the oppression of apartheid not only got to confront those who had done them wrong, but they were given voice and allowed to tell their stories of suffering and be heard. The commission's work helped set a tone of reconciliation in that country and aided their society in moving forward. Words and stories can be powerful in this way.

Today, as Trumpworld tries to shrink our national narrative and impose its own version of truth on the rest of us, it is more important than ever for all of us to find our voices and share our stories with each other.

Practice 6

Find Allies, Connect, and Build Community

DURING THE PAST YEAR, I have been a part of the Oregon Humanities Council's Conversation Project program. The goal of the program is to build community by getting people together in settings where they can talk, listen, and connect with each other through conversation. These reflective interactions are framed by a trained facilitator but are primarily open-ended dialogues about important topics and ideas, rather than being forums designed to find solutions or debate each other. Instead, the intention is to explore and learn with one another so that a sense of community can be built among those participating.

I have led conversations like this throughout the state of Oregon on the topic "Talking Values Across Political Divides." Each conversation has been rich as people go deep into their values, listen to each other, and try to understand where and how they connect as human beings, even if their politics and values differ. These settings are not about policy formation but about community formation.[1]

1. In April of this year, Oregon Humanities, which was formed in 1971 to distribute National Endowment for the Humanities (NEH) funds to public humanities projects across the state of Oregon, learned that they were losing their NEH funding, which accounts for 44 percent of their budget. This decision was made at the federal level by the new Department of Government

71

When we actively look for points of connection with others and make the time to have these kinds of interactions, we often find allies rather than enemies. And when we realize how we are connected as human beings, whether we see the world in the same way or not, we are able to build a sense of community. Mónica Guzman, in her wonderful book *I Never Thought of It That Way*, calls these type of interactions "bridging conversations" and provides her readers with a number of helpful tools to determine how best to connect with others and deepen relationships. Guzman concludes her useful insights by saying that "honesty, curiosity, and respect" are central to having conversations that can bridge our divides.[2]

A primary difficulty with Trumpworld is that many of those who are a part of it do not put a high value on listening but rather invest their time and energy in telling. Trumpworld is comfortable debating issues but not at ease with seeking out points of spiritual connection, which demonstrate our similarities as human beings. These tendencies are compounded by our current reality in which we feel more at ease with sound bites and don't take the time we need to ask people second questions or slow things down enough so that we can truly understand each other.

When Donald Trump proclaims that "we've ended the tyranny of so-called inclusion, equity, and diversity,"[3] he is saying in no uncertain terms that Trumpworld is not interested in creating bonds between each other on equal terms or in being open to the experiences of others who might come from different cultures or walks of life. It is difficult to make friends, let alone connect and build a sense of community, when you are not open to the stories, experiences, or values of those around you. This perspective is not only racist and classist, but it is dehumanizing as well. It is not to

---

Efficiency (DOGE), which was established by the Trump administration. This means that not only have staff been laid off, but also programs such as the Conversation Project and others that build community conversations among people from different walks of life will be in jeopardy. Davis, "DOGE Slashed Federal Humanities"; Oregon Humanities, "Federal Funding Cuts."

2. Guzman, *I Never Thought of It That Way*, 75, 234.

3. Grabenstein, "Trump Says."

say that "bridging conversations" are not possible, only that the investment must be thoughtful and mutual.

This is exacerbated by the fact that we are simply out of practice with taking the time to connect. Sure, we are on our phones and social media all the time, but are these connections about clicks and texts, or do they involve conversations that form deeper connections?

More often than not, people simply pass each other by on the streets, at work, and even at family gatherings. Perhaps COVID-19 and the isolation that resulted from that is partly to blame. Maybe our suburban lifestyles and busy schedules have finally caught up with us. No matter. The end result is that we seem less able to connect and build community with each other than was the case just a few years ago. Until we regain this ability, we will not be able to overcome the communal negatives that are an inherent part of Trumpworld.

Derek Thompson puts it well in his article "The Anti-Social Century," in the *Atlantic* magazine, when he asserts that our current anti-social behaviors are not serving us well: "Despite a consumer economy that seems optimized for introverted behavior, we would have happier days, years, and lives if we resisted the undertow of the convenience curse—if we talked with more strangers, belonged to more groups, and left the house for more activities."[4] While this would not be enough to overcome all the anti-social behaviors that are a part of the Trumpworld view of things, such actions would move us in the right direction.

Finding common ground, making connections, and building community require an openness to others, a willingness to listen, and a desire to understand. These things do not happen when only one perspective, opinion, or position is allowed. Yet Trumpworld often demands this kind of purity of thought.

Building human relationships requires an openness to other perspectives, as well as a willingness to apologize, forgive, and be humble, so that understanding and reconciliation can take place. This requires intention and hard work.

4. Thompson, "Anti-Social Century," 36.

When I think about forming alliances, seeking common ground, and the power of an apology and the potential of forgiveness to heal wounds and build a new future, I think about the time when US Congressman John Lewis and Elwin Wilson met in February 2009.

Wilson was one of the men who attacked and beat Representative Lewis bloody when he was a Freedom Rider traveling through a Greyhound bus station in Rock Hill, South Carolina. That event took place on May 9, 1961, and forty-eight years later Elwin Wilson went to visit Lewis in Washington, DC, to ask for forgiveness regarding what he had done. It was an act of intentional human connection.

Representative Lewis, who was a powerful US Congressmen by then, held no malice, felt no need for retribution, and had no desire to take revenge against Wilson. Instead, he listened and accepted his apology. Lewis met with Wilson four more times after that. This is what can happen through the power of reconciliation, which can only come about through a sincere, heartfelt apology and a genuine willingness to offer forgiveness in return.[5]

Wilson had held onto his sense of regret for nearly half a century but found the courage to do something about it. He wanted to experience healing from his past wrongdoing. Lewis met him on the human landscape of love, humility, and understanding and received him as a brother seeking wholeness and redemption.

Today the United States needs to find the courage to do this on many levels. This needs to happen between whites and Native Americans, African Americans, Hispanic Americans, and Asian Americans, among others, because great harm has taken place over the years, and the wounds of that remain a part of our collective story.

I witnessed the transforming power of this redemptive process on multiple levels in June 2018 at the Annual Conference session of the Oregon-Idaho United Methodist Church held in Boise, Idaho, and at the subsequent August 2018 ceremony surrounding the official presentation of the deed for a small parcel of property

5. Evans, "Asks Forgiveness," 1.

to the Nez Perce Executive Committee at the UMC Wallowa Lake Camp. "This land was part of the historic homeland of the Nez Perce people, taken from them in treaty violation" by the United States over a century before.[6]

For a number of months leading up to these events, the Camp and Retreat Ministries program of the United Methodist Church, under the leadership of Todd Bartlett, had been working on the return of some river property at the church's Wallowa Lake Camp to the Nez Perce Tribe. This was a natural next step toward human community and represented the UMC camping program's desire to continue its commitment of promoting friendship between the church and the Nez Perce people (or *Nimiipuu*, as the tribe is called in their native language).

The two groups have had a relationship since 2000 when the Nez Perce first began holding a Culture Camp at Wallowa Lake Camp for Nez Perce youth to learn the *Nimiipuu* language and culture from their elders. This annual event has been held under two flags: the United States flag and the flag of the sovereign nation of the Nez Perce Tribe.

The return of this small river parcel was an opportunity for the United Methodist Church to continue its relationship with the Nez Perce and deepen its connection. As Mary Jane Miles, a member of the Nez Perce Tribal Executive Committee, said at the land deed ceremony, "I never thought I would see a day come when we would have a hand of friendship from the larger community to the *Nimiipuu*."[7]

Initial impressions matter. Relationships matter. Intentions matter. Bishop Elaine Stanovsky, the bishop of the Greater Northwest Area, said at the time, "We experience the power of small acts to heal and transform us. Today was one of those moments."[8]

But there is more to this story. A few weeks earlier, when we gathered in Boise to commemorate the land's return to the Nez

6. Nelson, "Wallowa Lake Ceremony."
7. Nelson, "Wallowa Lake Ceremony."
8. Nelson, "Wallowa Lake Ceremony."

Perce, the church planned a ceremony to honor this August transfer of land. Everyone was touched by the experience.

Following this official ceremony, the schedule called for Duane Medicine Crow, the co-convener for the Oregon-Idaho Annual Conference's Committee on Native American Ministries, to make a presentation about the work of the past year. When Duane's opportunity to speak came, he decided to go in a different, more personal direction.

Duane, a member of the Crow Tribe, began by turning to the three elders who had come to the conference from the Nez Perce Executive Committee to participate in the land return ceremony. They were seated in the audience just in front of him. Duane looked directly at them and said that he wanted to make a public apology to the Nez Perce people for what happened in 1877.

In that year, the Crow Tribe participated in the campaign to capture Chief Joseph and his people as they attempted to flee from the US cavalry and escape across the Canadian border. The Crow Tribe's participation in that effort was important to the eventual capture of Chief Joseph and his people before they reached safety. Duane wanted the Nez Perce elders to know that he was sorry for what his ancestors had done.

Duane then walked from the podium into the audience and approached the table where the Nez Perce elders sat. He turned to them and proceeded to give his personal walking stick to one elder, his tobacco pouch to another, and the beaded necklace he was wearing to a third. The gathering of over four hundred participants, mostly white, was spellbound and sat in silence watching.

When Duane finished, Arthur Broncheau, one of the Nez Perce elders, thanked him for his kind words and gifts and then removed his own beaded necklace from around his neck and placed it over Duane's head. A profound apology had been given, received, and accepted. Forgiveness was returned. It was a sacred experience.

Since that day, I have often thought about what occurred— how it demonstrated how people are able to connect, how alliances are created, how community is formed, and how an apology and the spirit of forgiveness can transform everything. These kinds of human expressions are necessary in order for a community to be created that includes redemption and reconciliation. Without the humility of an apology and the grace of forgiveness, there can be no common ground among us.

What I have learned from Duane Medicine Crow is this: when you give something to someone else—whether it is a gift or an apology—it makes a difference if it comes from your essence rather than from your excess. There is a difference between these two things. One is transactional, the other relational and transformational. This work is not static but ongoing. It is what it means to find allies, connect with others, and build community.

Reverend Karen Hernandez, the UMC district superintendent for the region that includes the Wallowas, said, "As United Methodists, we have much work yet to do on our slow journey toward right relationships with the earth and the children of God. We are grateful that you (the Nez Perce leaders), in a gracious spirit of friendship, are willing to meet us here as we take a small step toward justice. It blesses us knowing that this land, which was never rightfully ours, is now in your hands."[9]

Reconciliation is ultimately about taking a series of small, but important, steps toward each other. It is about having the courage to apologize and the grace to forgive. It is about seeking common ground and forging alliances with others. These actions are not transactional in nature. They are deeply relational. They open up a world that is larger than tribe or nation, embracing the fullness of our humanity and establishing connections between us. John Lewis put it well when he said, "Forgiveness is profound. And it is a way forward—but first you must get out of your own way and allow for healing."[10]

Healing, apologies, and forgiveness do not come easily within the Trumpworld frame of reference. This is why it is so important for those of us committed to democracy to remember that these

9. Caldwell, "Blessing for Our People."
10. Lewis, *Carry On*, 90.

spiritual traits cannot be lost in the work we do, even when resistance and protest are involved.

Practice 7

Create a Mental Comfort Zone to Visit Regularly

WE ALL NEED AND often long for some kind of safe sanctuary where we can be ourselves, feel a sense of peace, renew our spirits, and find inner strength. For some of us, this is actually a specific location; for others it can be a place that we create and visit within our minds.

Where or what is that place for you?

For John Muir, it was Yosemite. For Claude Monet, it was Giverny. For Howard Thurman, it was the old oak tree in the backyard of his childhood home. For many, it happens through music or art or within one's own imagination.

Perhaps it is nothing more than a hot shower to start the morning or being still and quiet at the end of a long week or work day. Maybe it happens when you take time to pet your dog or cat or take a walk in nature. Having a special place does not depend on economics or on one's family situation, but in the end, it must be a place of personal freedom and sanctuary.

In each case, these special places connect us with our deeper selves and give us a sense of peace, creativity, and completeness. We all need places like this. Refuges. Sanctuaries. Havens. Places where we can be ourselves, feel safe, catch our breath, and be whole. Whatever the case may be, these are locales where we can go when we need relief from a hostile, troubling, chaotic world. We increasingly need such places today as Trumpworld disturbs the peace and causes chaos.

For me, one of these safe settings has always been Skyline Memorial Gardens outside of Portland. It is the cemetery on the hills overlooking the Tualatin Valley, where I grew up in Oregon and where much of my family is buried. It is a peaceful, beautiful place that anchors my spirit and reminds me of who I am and where I come from.

But I can also remember my drives through my community when I was in high school as being times of mental comfort. In college, whenever I'd fly home and pass over Mount Hood before flying down the Columbia River Gorge, I would often be in tears as I made my way home. I always felt a deep sense of peace during these times. Each of them served as a kind of sanctuary for me.

I'm clearly an Oregonian at heart, and those visual images reminded me of who I am. But I have also experienced some of the same feelings I do in these special locations when I hear John Lennon's *Imagine*, Leonard Cohen's *Hallelujah*, or Israel Kamakawiwoʻole's *Somewhere Over the Rainbow*, among others.

What are those special places in your life? We all need these personal havens. Places where we can be centered and mindful.

The Buddhist practice of focusing on one's breath during meditation is a useful way to center one's inner spirit and find a sense of peace in the world. It is so effective as a tool for calming one's spirit that a number of schools now use such mindfulness training as a way to help children address issues of anxiety, depression, and behavioral problems so they can focus better and learn more in the classroom. Some studies have shown that such techniques can even reduce aggression and violence in schools that use mindfulness training. Such techniques have also been shown to increase social engagement, emotional regulation, and a sense of optimism in students.[1]

---

1. Evans, "School Violence"; Kamenetz and Knight, "Embracing Mindfulness"; Liu et al., "School-Based Mindfulness."

Navigating Trumpworld is no different given the ability of those in power to inflict anxiety and suffering on unsuspecting people in sudden and damaging ways. Think immigrants, government workers, people living on the margins, those living along our borders, and those impacted by arbitrary trade wars and government funding decisions. People's plans, dreams, and livelihoods can be reduced to ashes without having any recourse, which obviously causes both real financial and emotional pain, as well as additional stress and anxiety. Once these external factors take hold, things can quickly spiral out of control, and we can be literally tied up in knots.

The practice of creating a mental comfort zone is not the ultimate solution to the problems that result from Trumpworld decisions since those actions can cause serious financial and material issues for those affected. But without having a place of peace and comfort within one's mind and heart, it is extremely difficult to maintain a sense of self and be able to function on a day-to-day basis.

We all need to find ways to be grounded and at peace with ourselves. The practice of mindfulness and centering is a critical part of this. Finding a comfort zone, a way to be centered and still, can serve as the anchor we need before returning to the chaos and distraction that marks Trumpworld.

This practice can be done on an individual basis, but it can also be something you do with a loved one. There is perhaps no more intimate and relaxing thing to do with another person than to lie quietly together and breath in harmony with each other. To feel the movement of another person's body as you take each breath is a wonderful experience of intimacy, connection, and wholeness. My wife, Susan, and I practice this regularly, and the results are both comforting and amazing.

Jon Kabat-Zinn, the founder of mindfulness-based stress reduction and author of *Coming to Our Senses, Mindfulness for Beginners,* and countless other books on the subject, put it this way: "Mindfulness is not one more thing you have to squeeze into your day, a task with some hoped-for outcome. . . . It's a love affair with the present moment, which is the only moment we're ever actually alive in, no matter how old or young we are."[2]

Whatever its form, our mental comfort zone must be a place where we can be ourselves and feel at home. It is the base camp we need to utilize as we confront a difficult, troubling world.

2. Kabat-Zinn and McLeod, "Power of Awareness," 67.

Practice 8

Know When Enough Is Enough

THE REALITY IS THAT I have a lot more material things than I need. That's true for many of us. I'm wealthier than a lot of people and poorer than many. While we live in a neighborhood where a number of individuals can't get their cars in the garage because they have too much stuff inside, we are among those who don't suffer from this problem. But we still face the same question that most Americans deal with: When is enough, enough?

You'd think that as Americans we'd be better at this than we are. After all, our country was founded on an idea—creating a nation based on life, liberty, and the pursuit of happiness—which has a number of spiritual values attached to it rather than merely materialistic ones.

In the early days, most people were just trying to forge a life that provided enough for their families and fostered a sense of stability and independence. The problem, however, is that we've gotten confused about what happiness is and where it can be found, and we live in an economic system that is more than happy to encourage us to buy and consume more than we need.

Capitalism requires constant sales and profit margins in order to succeed, flourish, and expand. And for many, "the chief business of the American people is business; they are profoundly concerned with producing, buying, selling, investing, and prospering in the world," as President Calvin Coolidge said in the 1920s.[1]

Sometimes I wonder if the United States wouldn't be better defined as a society of consumers rather than a nation of citizens. And as most of us know, the playing field isn't equal economically or politically for everyone.

While we pride ourselves on each individual having the right to vote, all you have to do is understand how the Supreme Court decision in *Citizens United* in 2010 has impacted our elections to realize that our laws now reflect our economic and election realities—money is a form of voice, and those with more money clearly have greater voice. In fact, those with money can and do buy political power and shape the destiny of the country on their own terms. While it used to be said that money talks, it is more accurate to say that money now has a political voice.

Some may say that this has always been true. All you have to do is consider the early southern plantations, later economic monopolies, or the Gilded Age. There have always been kings and queens and a ruling elite.

This may be true, but from the beginning our country had the audacity to claim that our political and economic ideals were based on a different, more equitable model in which democracy, equal rights, and an opportunity for all had replaced inherent inequality, wealthy elites, and the divine right of kings. The fact that slavery and economic inequality were baked into our founding reality is something that we still have not come to terms with, but in Trumpworld, this situation has been expanded on a scale unheard of for over a hundred years. Now, more is better, and those who need assistance are being disregarded, scorned, and neglected. Money buys access, and access buys power.

So how much is enough? And how should we use the material resources we possess? One way to respond to this question can be found in the words and actions of Andrew Carnegie, who in 1901 was considered the richest man in the world. However,

---

1. Terrell, "Not (Exactly) a Quote."

unlike his contemporary Gilded Age industrial barons, Carnegie vowed to give back to the community all he had earned:

> ... the duty of the man of Wealth: First, to set an example of modest, unostentatious living, shunning display or extravagance; to provide moderately for the legitimate wants of those dependent upon him; and after doing so to consider all surplus revenues which come to him simply as trust funds, which he is called upon to administer, and strictly bound as a matter of duty to administer in the manner which, in his judgment, is best calculated to produce the most beneficial results for the community— the man of wealth thus becoming the mere agent and trustee for his poorer brethren, bringing to their service his superior wisdom, experience, and ability to administer, doing for them better than they would or could do for themselves.[2]

While this attitude reflects a spirit of generosity, even if it simultaneously sounds paternalistic, the result of Carnegie's attitude toward his wealth resulted in the creation of twenty-five hundred libraries, schools, and other institutions, including Carnegie Mellon University in Pittsburgh and Carnegie Hall and a variety of foundations and funds that resulted in him giving away three hundred and fifty million dollars between 1901 and 1919.[3] While one can argue that Carnegie could have paid his workers a better wage or given more to the public good by paying more taxes, the reality is that he gave away a significant part of his wealth. This is something that many of his wealthy peers have not done over the years.

Much of Carnegie's giving was directed toward matters of education, following his belief that education could have a profound impact on one's life and prospects. For Carnegie, wealth didn't just mean having a sense of generosity with what one acquired; he believed it was a wealthy person's obligation to give his accumulated

2. Carnegie, *Essays and Other Writings*, 10.

3. Columbia University Libraries, "Philanthropy of Andrew Carnegie." This would be worth well over eleven billion dollars today.

resources away. In short, Carnegie understood when enough was enough.

This isn't always a concept that is easy to understand, and clearly it is not the prevailing view among the billionaires who are serving in the Trump administration. People who are wealthy are often overly concerned about money and things—think Trump and Musk, among many others—and feel the constant need to acquire more.

And even Bill Gates's recent decision to give away most of his wealth and close his foundation in twenty years reflects the challenges of contemporary generosity. Vice President J. D. Vance, who hasn't yet disclosed how he will give his riches away, said of Bill Gates's generosity that his foundation was one of the "cancers on American society" and that it was funding "radical left-wing ideology."[4] This is difficult to fully comprehend given that the Bill and Melinda Gates Foundation has maintained a significant and long-standing focus on global health. In any case, generosity has been added to the long list of cultural wars that are rudimentary to the Trumpworld view of reality.

But those with much less, even those who are quite poor, can also become preoccupied with money, wanting to make sure they simply have enough to survive. No matter what one's station in life is, money and things can easily gravitate to the center of one's life. But we all can learn to be generous with our resources no matter who we are.

One of the ways Susan and I tried to mitigate the focus on money for our children as young parents was when we introduced the idea of giving away some of our resources to charity throughout the year. We'd set aside some funds, and then together, as a family, each person reviewed the various requests for money we'd received during the year. Then, we'd decide where we'd like each portion of our family donations to go. It was a good way to spend time as a family thinking about the needs of others and the various issues that people were requesting money to pursue.

4. Kowitt, "Old Model," A11.

That said, the practice of knowing when enough is enough is especially important in combating the values of Trumpworld because Trumpworld immerses itself fully in materialism and wealth. And these are the key markers of success and accomplishment.

Consider how morally bankrupt it is for a sitting president of the United States to sell Bibles for $59.95, Trump Watches for $499, and coins with his face on them for $100. For Trump, there always seems to be a deal or profit to be made—whether economic or political—and this is seen as an asset, not a liability, in Trumpworld. In fact, Trump is hailed by many as being the "Dealmaker-in-Chief." True, being able to make good deals has its place in the world. In fact, at times it is something that we all try to do in one way or another.

But when everything in life becomes just another deal to be made, it's difficult to know what is really most important and of highest value. When money and material goods become the focus, deeper, spiritual values are simply no longer part of the equation. The irony of this is that there are always real, human costs and even significant losses involved in the equation, whether those factors are considered by those involved or not.

In a Trumpworld understanding of things, this way of relating to others spreads to everything else, from power to social privilege, since everything is considered transactional, and you simply can't have enough of whatever it is you want. Money, sex, and power all become commodities to be acquired, not resources and relationships to be stewarded with care and responsibility. In a fair and just society, wealth and power should not simply be merchandise but rather privileges to be held in trust and resources to be tended with great prudence.

The benchmark of progress cannot simply be determined on a material basis because there are always other factors involved. Remember the World Happiness Report referenced earlier? Material wealth does not always reflect personal or social happiness.

Consider the indicators of poverty. Researchers have determined that one of the leading indicators of poverty in the United States is a lack of human relationships, which often leads to economic instability, even homelessness. Relational, as well as material, factors influence success and happiness.

When we become more concerned about personal gain, wealth accumulation, and political power rather than spiritual capital and community well-being, we sacrifice human community and undercut the essence of a just society.

For those who want to anchor our country in a spiritual understanding of things, knowing when enough is enough is a critical part of maintaining a sense of moral grounding and spiritual centeredness. It often is an indicator of happiness and well-being. Not everything is a material transaction. How much do you need in order to be satisfied?

Practice 9

Practice Gratitude Daily

A KEY ELEMENT IN responding to the chaos, diminishment, and drama of Trumpworld is to have a regular rhythm to one's life that is positive. Nature is a good place to turn to when trying to establish this since there is an ongoing rhythm already in place within the natural world: day and night, dawn and dusk, the movement of four seasons. All of which give us a sense of wholeness and connection with our surroundings.

One of the ways in which I embrace these rhythms personally is through my early morning walks. It is a time to enjoy the natural world whether that means sun or rain, heat or cold. It is hard to be ungrateful when you take time to enjoy the world you are a part of. These walks are also a good time to silently let go and think about the things I am grateful for in life or to simply walk quietly and absorb creation's richness. This is why oftentimes when people are asked, "When do you feel closest to God?" they reply, "When I'm in nature." These places can serve as one's comfort zone.

The Buddhist monk Thich Nhat Hanh talks about the power of walking meditation in this way, saying, "You walk, and you do it as if you are the happiest person in the world. And if you can do that, you succeed in walking meditation." It is then that you learn that life and peace are available only in the present moment. But in order to experience this, you must slow down and stop running. He goes on to say that when you can say, "I have arrived. I am home. You understand that this is not a statement, but a practice and realization."[1]

This is something that we can own for ourselves, even when the world around us is full of negativity and chaos. We possess the power to walk in our own way and at our own speed. It was the Spanish poet Antonio Machado who put it this way, "There is no road, the road is made by walking."[2]

Trumpworld depends on chaos and keeping us running so that spirituality and sacredness go unnoticed, human connection is overlooked, the complexity of democracy is not understood, and a sense of gratitude is not achieved. A key response to this Trumpworld characteristic is to practice gratitude, which anchors us in a spirit of humility, wonder, awe, and connection. It is a revolutionary way to live one's life.

An example of this is my daily gratitude or blessing journal that has been a part of my life for nearly thirty years. This practice has played a central role in my life and is especially important now when so much of life is shrouded in negativity, hatred, and hostility toward others. I don't want these Trumpworld elements to consume my spirit and damage my soul.

While this practice has taken various forms over the years, keeping a blessing journal has always been a key part of my morning routine and has anchored my approach to each day.

It isn't difficult or complicated. It can be quite basic and rather simple. While the prompts for my journal entries have been different over time, the practice of doing this has transformed my life. Sometimes my practice has involved writing down one blessing from the previous day. Sometimes I've used the prompt of writing down a single word that I'd like to carry with me throughout the day. Sometimes I've listed special encounters I've had with others that I want to remember and savor. The prompt doesn't really matter, but the regular practice of it does. It has been a mainstay to my daily rhythm over the years and has changed who I have become.

1. Thich Nhat Hahn, "Walking Meditation" (from the audio titled "The Art of 'Slow Walking'").

2. Machado, *Fields of Castile*, 149.

Gratitude is a key element in living a spiritual life. It changes how one sees and experiences the world. It helps a person locate their place in the universe and realize we are a part of something grand and amazing. Gratitude humbles you and helps you appreciate and value the world in more profound ways, and it can be contagious.

Gratitude is also an antidote to division, antagonism, and hatred and is a critical component to one's resistance to the Trumpworld worldview. It is a good place to begin grounding one's response.

Practice 10

Be a Participant, Not a Bystander

REMEMBER "THE SNAKE" STORY I referenced earlier? The one in which Donald Trump told his audiences about the "silly old woman" who took home an injured snake as an act of compassion, only to have the snake bite and kill her?

Well, I've often wondered why, when Donald Trump told "The Snake" story to adoring crowds at one of his many campaign rallies, not a single Christian—not even a pastor or minister who had studied the Christian Scriptures and Jesus' parables—had the courage to stand up and say, "Wait a minute. There's something incorrect being communicated here. Jesus told a similar story, but his message was exactly the opposite of yours. Rather than fear and judge the stranger, the good Samaritan was deeply moved and offered compassion as he helped out someone who was in need from a different culture and background."

Instead, thousands of people at these rallies were more comfortable being bystanders and remaining silent. As a result, Trump's message of fear and judgment went unchallenged, allowing people to leave thinking, "I don't want to be stupid and offer aid to someone I don't know or who is in need; you might get hurt or even poisoned."

It is clear why so many hospitals are named after the good Samaritan centuries later. People have always been moved by the spiritual value inherent in compassion and what it means to offer assistance to those needing help. It is, after all, a very human thing to do, but this requires moving from the position of a bystander to becoming a participant.

I'm not sure there would have been many hospitals named "Don't Help Strangers, You Might Get Hurt." It doesn't have the same ring to it as "Good Samaritan," and I'm not sure anyone would go to one of those hospitals anyway!

In 1982, Susan and I first met and then traveled as international witnesses on behalf of the East Bay Sanctuary churches located in Berkeley/Oakland, California. We went there in order to be present in the Guatemalan and Salvadoran refugee camps along the Honduran border in the midst of the Central American wars. It was not only a difficult journey but also an unusual way to meet someone who would end up being my wife for over forty years!

Susan and I went there following the abduction of an American nurse and a Guatemalan doctor who had been serving as international workers at El Tesoro. It was a refugee camp in the countryside where hundreds of Guatemalans were located.

The day we arrived at the camp, the body of the doctor was found. He had been tortured before being killed. At the same time, while we were in Honduras, the American nurse happened to be testifying to a committee in the US Congress regarding what she had experienced.

One of my lasting impressions of that experience occurred when we met Ed, our contact in San Pedro Sula. Ed was to meet and travel with us by van to El Tesoro, but first we'd have dinner and spend the night in the city since the refugee camp was located along the border area.

As we walked down a street in San Pedro Sula and entered a restaurant for dinner, I could hear the vibrant conversations of those already inside. It was typical Latin American banter over a meal. As the three of us entered, we were seated at a corner table and given our menus.

Then a very memorable and disturbing thing occurred. Two men, wearing dark glasses, entered the restaurant and sat at a table in the corner across from us. Immediately, the conversations in the room stopped. It was as if a cone of silence had been placed over the space. The presence of these two men completely changed the atmosphere and mood of the room.

To this day, I am convinced that they were part of the Honduran paramilitary—perhaps even associated with those who had abducted the American nurse and ultimately killed the Guatemalan doctor. It's hard to know for sure. But what is clear is that those in the restaurant that evening in 1982 felt uncomfortable enough with these two men's presence that they stopped their conversations out of fear.

When we finished our dinner and left the restaurant, followed by the two men, we could hear the conversations resume inside the restaurant. These men had possessed the power to impose silence in their presence without saying a word. Things were evidently simply understood within that community.

Authoritarianism is like this. Over time, it has the power to change the atmosphere, alter social interactions, and even stop conversations. It can also change how we see each other, how we value each other, and how we treat each other. It can shatter dreams, change potential options, and deny people their basic rights.

A clear barometer for determining whether we are maintaining a sense of democracy or moving toward authoritarianism is this: in a country that sees itself as being "the land of the free and the home of the brave," everyone should feel free to express their opinions publicly without fear of reprisal or revenge. If we are truly a brave country, then anyone who speaks out should feel comfortable and have the courage to find their voice and use it in the public square. It is why whistleblowers have played such an important role in our society over the years. They have challenged power and shed light on dark secrets and inappropriate behaviors.

Another indicator of social health is when our news coverage highlights the views of many individuals, not simply the voice of one. When only one voice counts, we are making our way back to that restaurant scene in San Pedro Sula, where two men were able to shut down public conversation and impose silence through their presence. Authoritarianism depends on intimidation as a way of getting control over a society.

In many ways, we've reached the Dietrich Bonhoeffer moment in our own national history. What kind of society are we willing to live in? And, what role do we want to play in shaping it? Each individual has to answer these questions for themselves. It isn't an easy matter and requires thoughtful, soul-searching courage.

For Bonhoeffer, this occurred after his twin sister, Sabine, married a man with Jewish ancestry as the Nazis were rising to power. When her husband's father died, she asked her brother Dietrich to preach at the funeral. Dietrich declined. Afterwards, Bonhoeffer felt ashamed by his decision and wrote to his sister saying, "How could I have been so afraid at the time? All I can do is ask for you to forgive my weakness then."[1] It is often the case that we won't stand up to an unjust situation until it becomes personal.

Shortly after that, Bonhoeffer preached one of the first Christian sermons against the Nazis, calling for people to stand with the Jews. This was followed by a paper he wrote, saying that there were three possible ways for the church to respond to the Nazis: (1) it can challenge the state by asking if its actions are legitimate, (2) it can aid the victims of state action—and Bonhoeffer says that the church has an unconditional obligation to do this—and (3) the church can do more than just aid the victims of the wheel of state; it can jam a spoke into the wheel.

While there is a role for people to play in each of these options, Dietrich Bonhoeffer chose to sacrifice his life for the latter one. We each have these same alternatives to consider as well, whether we are Christians or not. What role will we play when injustice and cruelty prevail and we are witnesses to it?

Going against the grain of political power is not easy. At the time of the American Revolution, there were the Tories, who preferred colonialism to independence. At the time of the American Civil War, there were those who wanted to preserve slavery rather than support freedom and equality for all. Today there are

1. Doblmeier, *Bonhoeffer*, 36 min.

those who don't see anything wrong with the values and practices of Trumpworld, even while there are others who believe that the American ideals of life, liberty, and the pursuit of happiness for all, not just for some, are at risk.

It is always a challenge to move from being a bystander to becoming an activist, but history is filled with examples of people who have done this.

The American literary community, including the likes of Sinclair Lewis, Jack London, and Robert Penn Warren, used their writing skills to stand up to Huey Long, who was using his power in an authoritarian manner in Louisiana as fascism was rising in America in the 1930s. Edward R. Morrow, the great American journalist, took on Joseph McCarthy at the height of his power and influence when he was maliciously attacking and denouncing Americans in the 1950s.

Maria Resa, the Filipino journalist and winner of the Nobel Peace Prize, did a similar thing when she stood up to President Duterte in her home country in recent years. She was following in the footsteps of Ninoy Aquino and later his wife, Corazon, and eventually millions of fellow Filipinos who stood up to President Ferdinand Marcos in the 1980s and eventually brought his dictatorship to an end.

In recent years, there has been a significant number of women who have stood up and revealed the many ways in which they personally experienced sexual abuse, aggression, and other inappropriate behavior. There was a large enough group who did this that they were able to create the MeToo movement and successfully prosecute these abuses against a number of men in positions of power.

Just as the spirit moves in an inward-out direction, changing from being a bystander to becoming a participant involves a movement from the personal to the social realm. It is a movement from one's conscience to one's social practice.

But there are countless examples of others who have used their skills to stand up against dictators and authoritarians across the globe. There are the inspiring stories of Nelson Mandela in

South Africa, Eunice Paiva in Brazil, Oscar Romero in El Salvador, and the Mothers of Plaza de Mayo in Argentina as well—people from all walks of life who moved from being bystanders to becoming activists in order to preserve the values that opposed authoritarianism and affirmed democracy. Sometimes these individuals did so at great cost to themselves.

And yet, we frequently stay on the sidelines and say to ourselves, "Who am I? What difference can I make in the lives of others? The problems before us are just too big for someone like me to do anything."

This kind of self-doubt makes me think about Barry. Barry lived on the streets of Portland, Oregon for many, many years and was houseless. He struggled with mental health issues but was also deeply compassionate and had a laser-focused interest in matters of social justice. Most importantly, Barry used the resources he had at his disposal—his voice, his passion for life, and his bicycle—to show up everywhere for a variety of causes and events. You'd see Barry at a political rally. You'd see him at classes and lectures involving nearly every religious tradition. You'd see Barry at city council meetings sharing his views, giving public input to one local concern or another.

By the time of his death in 2023, Barry was an icon in the city. No wonder when he died over two hundred people, representing an interfaith community of Lutherans, Unitarians, United Methodists, Quakers, Jews, and Buddhists, came together to celebrate his life. Barry refused to play the part of a bystander and instead lived his life as a participant who was filled with a deep sense of compassion and justice, even though he had little in the way of material wealth. Barry made a difference with his life, and his presence is still missed by those he touched.

Today in the United States, we are, like Germany in the 1930s, at a critical decision point in our history, and Dietrich Bonhoeffer is confronting us with the same challenge that he posed to people of faith back then.

Now we must decide whether preserving democracy is worth our time and energy or whether we will remain on the sidelines and let those who want to be dictators and advance authoritarian rule in this new era have their way.

Donald Trump and those who share power with him want us to fear risking our time, resources, and energy on behalf of others. They see the world as a place of scarcity rather than being rich with abundance. The Trumpworld perspective counts on the privatization of everything at the expense of public resourcing and investment. This allows those with power and wealth to get richer, while the general public loses agency and we become consumers rather than citizens. When this happens, our choices have been made for us, and we become bystanders.

But the truth is that we all have agency, resources, and power available to us. This can take the form of everything from financial resources and political power to simply recognizing and encouraging others when we encounter them. Yes, I see you. You have worth and dignity. It can mean volunteering your time, providing a listening presence to someone who is struggling, being a supportive grandparent, or doing political advocacy on behalf of a candidate or cause. The list is endless.

The choice is ours to make.

Practice 11

Be Constructively Passionate and Use the Power You Possess

It may sound rather basic, but we are all human beings first and foremost. Until we appreciate this reality, however, it is hard to create a lasting, just society because we simply won't honor or make room for each other. When that happens, things end up like they do in George Orwell's *Animal Farm*. The social revolution starts out fine, just like it does for the animals when they overthrow their human oppressors—all animals are considered equal. But once the pigs gain total control of the farm, things change. Then it becomes a situation in which "all animals are equal, but some animals are more equal than others."[1]

Sound familiar? It's what happens when you don't honor diversity, deny a sense of equity, and stop being inclusive. When this happens within a society, animal or otherwise, everyone is equal, but some are considered more equal than others.

In Trumpworld, things start out on an unequal basis from the very beginning—some are the right kind of people, others not so much, so the social order can only get worse from there. We all have a role to play in creating a foundation of genuine equality, and that foundation begins by us seeing everyone as being an equal,

1. Orwell, *Animal Farm*, 134.

or as Jesus taught, "Love your neighbor as yourself" (Mark 12:31, from Lev 19:18).

The truth is that each one of us has a unique set of interests, skills, and abilities, so there is a place for all of us to contribute to society. In order to do this, however, we must discover not only our own distinct voice but also determine what we are passionate about and what gives us life.

Being passionate and alive is contagious, and the world longs for this kind of positive energy, especially today. At the same time, we must be in touch with the world enough to understand the realities we face as a society so we can apply our time and energy in worthwhile ways. This is part of the dance that takes place between our personal and social worlds.

Most all of us have jobs to do in order to survive, but it is through our vocations that we truly thrive and make our mark on the world. It is at the intersection of these pursuits that we discover what Frederick Buechner understood when he said, "[Your vocation in life] is the place where your deep gladness and the world's deep hunger meet."[2]

On one level, I'd like to believe that if we would just be kind to each other, as Mr. Rogers used to teach the children watching his show, then everything would take care of itself and be fine. While being kind is a great beginning, it simply isn't enough to make all the changes that are needed today. Expressing kindness to each other might resolve a number of our current problems, but there still would be so much more work left to do in our country. The world is simply too complex for kindness to be our only response.

There are children who are hungry or who have been neglected, people who have recently lost their jobs or who have been unemployed for far too long, and there are immigrants who need to be attended to as they seek to make our country their home and offer their unique skills and abilities to life here. There are those who have been displaced by one kind of natural disaster or another and those who simply can't make ends meet.

2. Buechner, *Wishful Thinking*, 119.

There are those struggling with mental or physical illnesses and those who have been subjected to racism and prejudice their entire lives. Lots of people feel isolated, alienated, or simply left behind. In short, there are a host of needs confronting us as we try to bind up wounds, heal our collective social problems, and move forward to create a kinder, more just society.

Whatever actions one chooses to undertake, the statement attributed to Mother Teresa that "not all of us can do great things, but we can do small things with great love" is helpful guidance in how we should proceed. This is why the work in front of us is first and foremost about developing a healthy spirituality. It is what makes love possible. Most of the actions that are needed must be anchored in basic spiritual principles so they can help us change the atmosphere in which we are living. These principles include things like kindness, love, compassion, generosity, and justice.

It is in this way that the harshness and cruelty of the prevailing Trumpworld dynamics can be overcome, and it's how we can put our lives back together. As they say, "This isn't rocket science." But it is most assuredly about the fundamentals of spirituality.

While most of us are involved in the dynamics of a career, raising a family, and making ends meet, it is still possible in whatever situation we find ourselves to take the time needed to greet others, express kindness, and demonstrate compassion. At the same time, in order to make a difference, it is important to know what you are passionate about and what tools you have at your disposal so you can use your agency and resources in positive ways in the larger community.

Some of us will need to focus our attention on working with children, those who are marginalized, and those who are living without homes. Do you have a gift of music or art or conversation or business or teaching? What settings are you most comfortable working in—senior centers, schools, in political campaign offices, or with computers? There are thousands of directions one could go in. Which one is right for you and makes you feel most alive?

We are living at a time in which the world's needs are being revealed in a multitude of ways, and our task is to find the intersections between those needs and our passions and abilities. And Trumpworld is seemingly adding new dimensions to this list on a regular basis.

But Howard Thurman reminds us that what we ultimately choose to do with our time and skills is up to us. In his words, "Don't ask what the world needs. Ask what makes you come alive, and go do it. Because what the world needs is people who have come alive."[3]

Wherever you find yourself in the social order, there is work to be done. Some of that work has to do with our actions, but all of it has to do with how we view and treat others, how we use the power we have, and how our efforts contribute to the greater whole.

Now is the time to discover your passion, assess your talents and skills, and invest in a future not only for yourself but for society as a whole. As many have said before, "We are the ones we have been waiting for."

3. Quoted in Bailie, *Violence Unveiled*, xv.

Practice 12

Remain Curious
and Remember the Children

RICK STEVES, THE WELL-KNOWN travel guru, says that "we travel in order to learn from culture shock."[1] What Steves is highlighting is the fact that travel should take us outside of ourselves, our assumptions, and our normal ways of doing things. That's how we grow and learn, and travel is a great way to do that.

In his book *The Art of Travel*, Alain De Botton says,

> What, then, is a travelling mind-set? Receptivity might be said to be its chief characteristic. Receptive, we approach new places with humility. We carry with us no rigid ideas about what is or is not interesting. . . . Home, by contrast, finds us more settled in our expectations. . . . We have become habituated and therefore blind to it.[2]

I always learn best when I find myself on the edge. By this, I mean being in situations in which I experience differences, new assumptions, and contrasting views. This usually happens, as Alain De Botton says, when we have a traveling mindset and are immersed in a new reality of some kind. This could occur when we travel, when we find ourselves in a different cultural situation, or simply when we notice and are willing to explore the differences that are

1. Podplesky, "Rick Steves Shares Lessons."
2. De Botton, *Art of Travel*, 242–43.

a part of our current realities. When we are curious, we tend to be receptive.

When I worked as a seminary intern at the Cuernavaca Center for Intercultural Dialogue on Development (CCIDD) in Mexico in 1981, I told the North American groups that came to the center that their primary challenge would be to fully immerse themselves in the cross-cultural experiences that were a part of the program in such a way that they would actually leave the United States. This would require setting aside their preconceived assumptions, opinions, and judgments long enough to enter someone else's lived reality.

That's what an immersion experience is all about. Otherwise, in this case, we would find ourselves being physically located in Mexico but unable to actually learn from a rural farmer or the ex-iled government figure or a frightened refugee as they shared their stories. Our preconceived notions would simply get in our way.

Perhaps it could be said that the mark of a good life, like the experience of good travel, depends on being curious and open to exploring things outside of ourselves. This, as De Botton says, requires a kind of humility that is not always present in our day-to-day life.

Traveling and crossing cultural boundaries not only help us grow, but these experiences shape the worldviews we form and the kind of communities we create. It is why democratic principles are so foundational to community life. They embrace the reality of our differences and create settings where those differences can be ap-preciated and valued.

There are simply too many experiences, perspectives, opin-ions, and approaches for one to narrow one's worldview to a single point of reference, as authoritarianism is prone to do. Mónica Guzman puts it well in *I Never Thought of It That Way*: "Curiosity requires uncertainty and uncertainty requires flexibility."[3] This is why experiences such as travel and stepping outside one's usual patterns are so rich in terms of personal growth and democratic

---

3. Guzman, *I Never Thought of It That Way*, 138.

health—we are forced to become less rigid and more flexible, which is a necessary trait in free and open societies.

Trumpworld replaces this spirit of curiosity and openness with a dependence on fear, suspicion, threat, and closedmindedness. The very nature of the public good and the sense of compassion that is shown in the story of the good Samaritan we mentioned earlier are simply too difficult to comprehend in a Trumpian worldview.

Why would anyone go out of their way to understand someone else's experience or lend aid without getting anything in return? The answer begins with curiosity—and a willingness to go outside of one's own limited understandings in order to appreciate life more fully from another point of view or render assistance to someone who is different from you.

Contrast an approach based on curiosity and an appreciation of others' life experiences with what is embodied in Project 2025 and those from the Trump administration who participated in its formulation. Not only is it an 887-page road map to a very narrowly defined vision of America, but nearly all of those involved from the Trump administration who participated in its formulation and implementation were white men. The result is the production of a document that dislodges women from decisions regarding their own bodies, privatizes government functions allowing them to be controlled by those with wealth, and narrowly defines who can be considered an American, with a clear bias against those who come from other countries and those who are not white.

This isn't to say that white men should not have a voice in the public arena, but when only one voice or viewpoint is included in the formation of public policies Project 2025 is what you end up with. This is simply not a broad, inclusive, or deep enough blueprint for a nation as diverse as ours is. In the end, the governed need a government that looks and sees the world from more than one vantage point.

This is why authoritarianism demands conforming to a strict ideology. Ideology is not comfortable with two-way conversations, let alone with listening to someone else's real-life experiences or points of view. That would mean a loss of power and control, and dictatorships are about declarations and denunciations, not about building community together.

Building authentic community requires conversations and the use of open-ended questions. It is why the art of the second question is so vital to human understanding. "Tell me more about that." "What does that experience mean to you?" "Have you had this feeling before?" "If you could do it all again, what would you do differently?" Ultimately, this kind of exploration has to be mutual for these conversations to contribute to real, authentic community.

In the 1940s, E. Stanley Jones, the great Christian missionary who was a close personal friend of Mahatma Gandhi's, created Faith Roundtables in India. One of the principles of these roundtables required those attending—Christians, Hindus, and Muslims—to speak only about their own personal experiences of faith, not about religious tenets or doctrines. It was Jones's way of making those conversations personal rather than ideological. It also created an atmosphere of curiosity rather than one of judgment.

While the world is an evolving, expansive place, populated with a rich array of cultures and points of view, Trumpworld shrinks the real world and in the process isolates the United States, and especially white Americans, from other people and perspectives under the guise of "Make America Great Again." There is nothing great about being ignorant of different points of view or cultural expressions. This narrow-minded approach to living and learning inhibits spiritual growth and diminishes community life.

How do you express your curiosity? How do you travel outside your comfort zones? What cultures or points of view do you want to learn more about? These explorations are the basis for lifelong learning.

I have been fortunate in my educational experience to be blessed with the opportunity to learn from a variety of points of view, starting by going to the Claremont Colleges in the 1970s. Claremont is a cluster of adjacent colleges that are independent of each other yet allow students to take classes at each of them. While I was a student at Claremont Men's (McKenna) College, I attended classes at the other schools as well, and this experience enriched my educational learning tremendously.

Each school had its own history and perspective, and I benefited from this, learning from liberals and conservatives, those from a strictly scientific background and those who were people of deep religious faith. My assumptions and prior beliefs were always challenged in the classroom, as multiple perspectives enriched my learning. It was an example of a liberal arts education at its best.

I had a similar experience in seminary in the 1980s. As a United Methodist, I attended most of the schools associated with the Graduate Theological University in the San Francisco Bay Area, even though I went to San Francisco Theological Seminary, which was Presbyterian. I learned from Jesuits, Dominicans, Franciscans, Baptists, Episcopalians, and others as a part of that experience. Again, it was through encountering an array of differences rather than from a single dominant point of view that I gained a deeper understanding of spirituality.

These prior learning settings helped prepare me for the extraordinary experience of attending the Parliaments of World Religions in Melbourne, Australia (2009), and Toronto, Canada (2018). Imagine a single setting in which thousands of faith leaders from countless religious traditions and dozens of countries came together to share and learn from each other. These were two unforgettable experiences, but if you weren't curious and open to exploring what you encountered, you would have missed the whole thing.

Thinking about these remarkable opportunities reminds me of the time when President John F. Kennedy said to a group of Nobel Prize winners at a White House dinner:

> I think this is the most extraordinary collection of talent, of human knowledge, that has ever been gathered at the White House, with the possible exception of when Thomas Jefferson dined alone. Someone once said that Thomas Jefferson was a gentleman of thirty-two, who

> could calculate an eclipse, survey an estate, tie an artery,
> plan a cause, break a horse, and dance the minuet.[4]

And yet, for all Jefferson's brilliance, he too had significant blind spots in his worldview regarding matters of slavery and human dignity, which meant that his lack of curiosity in some areas of his life limited his understanding of others and ultimately stunted his spiritual development.

This illustration of someone as brilliant as Jefferson just demonstrates that an open spirit and a willingness to learn must always have the capacity to wake us up so that we can be aware of others' experiences and perspectives, lest we limit our understanding of life. How different Jefferson's understanding might have been if he had taken the time to learn about the lives and perspectives of those who were his slaves. Curiosity is an ever-expanding circle, and once we stop asking questions or fail to look at life through the vantage point of others, our understanding begins to shrink.

This is why seeing our present moment, with all its trials and tribulations, not only from the diverse perspectives of our time but also through the lens of history and the point of view of future generations, is so important. We have an obligation to our ancestors who passed the baton to us to carry forward the democratic traditions that we have inherited, but we have an obligation to those generations who will follow after us as well. When we do our part and open our viewpoint up beyond the present moment in which we are living, our perspective will naturally expand. Seeing life in terms of the future is an important part of our responsibility to those who will follow after us.

This outlook begs the question: What do the children think about who we are and how we behave? What do they think when they witness Donald Trump's behavior toward others or when they watch the January 6 insurrection at the US Capitol or when their neighbors are detained or deported to detention centers far away? What does that teach our children about the nature of government or how to go about treating others as you'd like to be treated

---

4. Purdy, "Extraordinary Presidential Statement."

yourself? How do the current public policies impact the schools they attend, the friends they play with, or their view of themselves? What values will they carry with them as they become adults?

I think about what I learned from my own parents regarding compassion, kindness, generosity, and love and wonder to myself where and how those values are being taught to upcoming generations. I think about the children of people from different races and cultures and wonder what their dreams are and how they will discover and share their voices in the world. I'm curious about such things and hope that we are providing the kind of foundations that future generations can count on in order to navigate the world we are creating for them.

While we should be aware of the impact of our decisions on the children in our midst, at the same time, we need to listen to their voices to see what their perspectives and interests are regarding the issues of our day. There are many articulate young voices speaking out today, expressing their opinions about a variety of current issues and challenging adult leaders who often don't seem to be worried about the future in the same way.

I think about the students from Marjory Stoneman Douglas High School in Parkland, Florida, who spoke out forcefully following the mass shooting that took place there in 2018. I think about Greta Thunberg, who is a global leader on climate change matters and has said, "When we look back at this crucial time, we want to be able to say that we did everything we possibly could to push in the right direction. And while we young people may not be able to vote or make decisions in today's society, we have something just as powerful. Our voices."[5]

In times such as these, we need to encourage and assist the children and use whatever power we have to surround them with love and give them space to utilize their voices. One way we can do this is by supporting the natural urge of children to be curious. We can do this best by modeling curiosity ourselves.

5. Thunberg, *No One Is Too Small*, 119.

Epilogue

A Call to Action

A dangerous ambition more often lurks behind the specious mask of
zeal for the rights of the people than under the forbidding appearance
of zeal for the firmness and efficiency of government. History will
teach us that the former has been found a much more certain road to
the introduction of despotism than the latter, and that of those men
who have overturned the liberties of republics, the greatest number
have begun their career by paying an obsequious court to the people,
commencing demagogues and ending tyrants.

—Alexander Hamilton

TODAY, MANY PEOPLE FEEL politically homeless, socially isolated,
and spiritually adrift. How can we regain a sense of healthy political movement, overcome our sense of isolation, and ground ourselves spiritually?

In short, many feel like their backs are up against a wall and
don't know where or how to turn in a different, healthier direction.
My hope is that *Navigating Trumpworld* has provided you with a
spiritually grounded pathway forward. There is a lot of work to
be done on both a personal and social level in order for us to get

where we need to be as a democratic society, and this work will take time. It will require us all to work together.

In 1949, when Howard Thurman wrote his landmark book *Jesus and the Disinherited*, he said that he wrote it for "those who need profound succor and strength to enable them to live in the present with dignity and creativity."[1] As one reads Thurman's work, it is clear that he was writing to those who he felt had their backs up against a wall.

Thurman wanted to provide a way forward that was spiritually grounded and ethically sound in order to confront the issues of his day, including racism. In the book, he goes on to address what he calls "the religion of Jesus" and how it has often been used by those with power and position against those who have been disinherited for one reason or another by society. He points out how ironic it is that Jesus spent much of his life among the disinherited, and yet his message has often been hijacked by those that Jesus often called out for their cruelty and faithlessness.

Thurman felt that in order to make progress in an unjust world, those who had their backs up against a wall would need to avoid what he called "the hounds of hell," those lurking inner demons of fear, hypocrisy, and hatred.[2] By avoiding them, Thurman believed that it was possible to respond to oppression, fear, hypocrisy, and hatred in a spiritually grounded, ethically principled manner.

No wonder it is said that Dr. Martin Luther King Jr. carried a copy of *Jesus and the Disinherited* with him during the civil rights struggles. Thurman's words provided him with inspiration and guidance along the way. We would be wise to remember Thurman's lessons now as we respond to the dynamics of Trumpworld. After all, the list of those who are "wall-bruised" today continues to expand as more Trump policies are put into place.

How appropriate it is that one of Donald Trump's main ambitions in his first administration was to build a wall along the southern border and use language and rhetoric to construct artificial

1. Thurman, *Jesus and the Disinherited*, 11.
2. Thurman, *Jesus and the Disinherited*, 29.

walls between Americans. Dividing people in one way or another from each other is a hallmark of authoritarian rule, and building walls is a cornerstone to a Trumpworld understanding of life.

Today, many of us are in need of a new kind of succor and strength so that we too can live with a sense of dignity and creativity.

We are living at a time when a complete reordering of the American political scene and our cultural norms is taking place on a grand scale. It is happening in a systematic and alarming manner that will ultimately destroy many of our social institutions and eventually unravel our unique democratic history. Left unchecked, we will soon lose track of the principles that have served us well over the years.

This reality is seen most clearly by examining the specifics that are a part of Project 2025 and probing how the beliefs undergirding this document are being implemented by the Trump administration as national policy. As we have discussed throughout this book, when political decisions about how community life is organized impact the nature of public trust, determine who is seen as being legal and acceptable and who is not—whose stories are valued and whose are dismissed—and establish invasive limits on the personal decisions one is able to make regarding their own health and well-being, then the spiritual fabric of a society is affected and altered as well.

In addition, when the goal of policy formation is to actually "villainize" civil servants, as Russell Vought (the current White House budget director) has said, so that they will resign and steps are taken to traumatize immigrant families seeking safety and employment in the United States, then we are actually creating a different kind of society with a different set of spiritual values. Who we are, not just what we do, changes in a fundamental way when this is part of one's worldview.

As a result, the current dangers to American life that are embedded in Trumpworld not only have to do with matters of democracy versus authoritarianism but also with the spiritual principles that are put in place when certain policies are enacted. This crossover from the political to the spiritual realm occurs when power is used and abused in such a way that the diversity of the community is no longer considered, only the creation of a specific kind of reality.

As we've discussed throughout this book, democracy is about openness and transparency, conversation and diversity of opinion, trust and civility. Authoritarianism and despotism depend on conformity and revenge, single-mindedness and loyalty, fear and judgment. This is why our founders set up a complex system of checks and balances in order to prevent authoritarianism from happening and avoid the return of the "divine right of kings" in the United States.

Today, we are experiencing a number of dramatic challenges that have only taken place occasionally in the history of our nation. The difference this time is that, unlike the late eighteenth century when the best minds in America gathered at Independence Hall in Philadelphia to sign the Declaration of Independence and adopt the Constitution, today the reordering of power and privilege is taking place in the White House at the hands of one man, Donald Trump, and his associates, who are making executive rather than legislative decisions about the future of our country.

These wholesale changes favor those with wealth and power rather than making any attempt to gather the various interests of a diverse country and shape those varied interests into one, united nation. There is a fundamental difference between *E pluribus unum*, "out of many one," and the notion of me first.

Each time we witness a cruelty that goes unchallenged, each time we observe something that is fundamentally wrong or illegal and say nothing, each time we see someone being dehumanized and no one comes to their aid, our common humanity is diminished. Yet this is precisely what is happening today, and we must insert ourselves into this unfolding drama (i.e., the wheel of state that Bonhoeffer spoke about) by staying informed, speaking up, protesting, and organizing. It is time to participate in the kind of "good trouble" that John Lewis often advocated.

Good trouble involves political tactics, such as rallies and letter writing, boycotts, donations, and other forms of active resistance. In the end, these tactics must be grounded in a deeper, spiritual strategy, like the ones outlined in this book, for them to have a lasting impact and help us shape the kind of world we want to ultimately live in.

First and foremost, it means making sure that you minimize the damage Trumpworld does to your own spiritual life. This is why so many of the practices I've outlined matter so much. If we cannot maintain our own spiritual integrity and well-being, it will be nearly impossible to survive what is taking place in the political realm, let alone thrive as healthy, happy human beings. Now is a time to develop and express a liberating spirituality that can contend with the negative narrative that Trumpworld depends on.

The reality is that President Trump simply can't help himself. He is not self-reflective. He lacks genuine compassion. He appears to be unfamiliar with the basic practices that are involved in living a spiritually grounded life. As a result, his inner life has become deformed and unstable.

As I said in practice 1, life moves in an inward-out manner. While this is true, there is also a natural dance that takes place between what is private and what is public, between the spiritual world and the material world.

Currently, this dance is taking place in a profound and troubling manner, requiring our best and most thoughtful spiritual response. One thing is certain: there is a lot at stake as Trumpworld continues to be in control of our national attention and agenda. The consequences of this reality have already had a lasting impact on our nation, but the final outcome is still a work in progress.

I grew up when the State of Oregon was under the leadership of a political visionary, Governor Tom McCall, who was a Republican from a different era. During his years in office, the Beach Bill was enacted, making all Oregon beaches public, the Bottle Bill was adopted, advancing the cause of recycling in the state, land use planning was set in motion, and groups such as the Thousand

Friends of Oregon and SOLV were created and became active in the state's public policy.

These various public initiatives not only shaped the political landscape of the state, but they had a deep impact on the spiritual life of others as well, demonstrating how one's government and leaders can help shape the destiny of its citizens. Governor McCall was skillful enough to balance economic growth with environmental protection and do so in a way that inspired an entire state. It became known as "the Oregon story."

I was also influenced at a young age by the inspiring words of President John F. Kennedy, who said, "Ask not what your country can do for you—ask what you can do for your country," and Dr. Martin Luther King Jr., who dreamed of a better day for his children where "they will not be judged by the color of their skin but by the content of their character."[3]

At the time, such proclamations moved our nation and thousands of people went into public service as a result, while the opportunities for people of all races, cultures, and genders continued to expand. These were difficult but heady days, when public life was a place where positive values and future thinking took hold, and our government responded to rather than dictated the values of the people. We must not give up this ground, even as it is under attack.

A new generation of leaders and the active involvement of those who took to the streets in a different era must now combine forces and enter the political world armed with the spiritual resources necessary to withstand the Trumpworld mentality and worldview while also bringing to the fore a politics that works from inside out and that is open, collective, and curious.

It is still unclear what this response will ultimately look like, but it can only take shape when we stop being bystanders and instead take action.

So, where do we go from here?

The first thing to remember is that in a democracy we all have a role to play, and as the twelve practices I've outlined indicate, we

---

3. National Archives, "Inaugural Address"; NPR, "I Have a Dream."

can both honor our spirituality and utilize it effectively in ways that impact the future direction of our country. But we must be focused. We must be intentional. We must be spiritually oriented. We must be strategic. And even the small things matter.

In my family, values, public service, and community have always been held in high regard. I have two brothers, Mark and Gordon. The three of us grew up in a very special, loving family in which we were each given the freedom and support we needed to pursue our dreams and interests. Each of us headed in our own unique direction, but our parents were there for us with encouragement and love. But they let us each make our own decisions.

Our parents came from very different backgrounds themselves. Our mom came from a loving, closely knit Swedish family that immigrated to the United States in the nineteenth century. Our dad was raised in a family that struggled a good deal on the margins. Our dad's father dealt with alcoholism and financial instability. His mom ended up marrying three times over the course of her life. His brother was killed at a young age while traveling on a train. So, our dad had much to overcome within his own family system in order to reach a place of stability and direction. But through determination, a commitment to discipline, and his deep dedication to family and community, our dad and mom were able to create a sense of stability and extend it to their children. Mark, Gordon, and I were the beneficiaries of those investments.

As brothers, we learned these lessons well, and they shaped the values we developed and the ways in which we have lived our lives. This is not to say that it is simply a matter of focus, commitment, and hard work. Society has placed a variety of barriers in people's way, and those barriers have not been equally distributed, as racism, bigotry, and economic inequality factor into the equation. But it is to say that all of us must be mindful of the role we play in our collective destiny, and this occurs on a moment by moment basis and has to do with how we view the world and how we treat ourselves and others.

My favorite image of my brother Gordon is when I was visiting his family in Brazil in 1979. A group of us had just completed our work as a mission team, and I was traveling with Gordon just before returning home.

When we got to a local bus station to change buses, there was another American standing on the bus platform. He was obnoxious and rude toward those around him. One might say he was acting like an "ugly American."

As Gordon and I witnessed this individual's actions and I proceeded to board the bus to leave for the airport, I looked out the window and saw Gordon approaching the gentleman. I immediately knew what was going to happen next. This man was going to have an encounter with my brother, and as a result, he would end up gaining a greater insight into Brazilian culture and a better understanding of how he was being perceived as an American. I knew that Gordon would use the resources he had at his disposal to make a difference in that situation rather than simply be a bystander.

At the same time, one of my favorite images of my brother Mark has to do with how he and his wife, Helena, who is from the Czech Republic, utilize their apartment in Prague when they are at home in Oregon. Following the invasion of Ukraine by Russia, they decided to make their apartment available to a Ukrainian refugee family when they weren't living there, choosing to use the resources they have at their disposal for the benefit of others.

Real change is a difficult thing to come by, especially when democracy is involved. It takes individuals—lots of them—to become engaged. Leaders can move the hearts and minds of people, but in the end, real change involves all of us. We each play a role in the outcome of our national narrative.

Derek Thompson put it this way: "No one can say precisely how to change a nation's moral-emotional atmosphere, but what's certain is that atmospheres do change. Our smallest actions create norms. Our norms create values. Our values drive behavior. And our behaviors cascade."[4]

4. Thompson, "Anti-Social Century," 38.

In 1968, at another critical time in our nation's history, Robert Kennedy put it well when he said in his book *To Seek a Newer World*,

> Our future may lie beyond our vision, but it is not completely beyond our control. It is the shaping impulse of America that neither fate nor nature nor the irresistible tides of history, but the work of our own hands, matched to reason and principle, that will determine destiny. There is pride in that, even arrogance, but there is also experience and truth. In any event, it is the only way we can live.[5]

This is the task before us today, and it is up to us to take up this challenge. There are no others waiting in the wings. I hope and pray that you will join me in this struggle. The future of our country and the promise of democracy will depend on it.

5. Kennedy, *To Seek a Newer World*, 235.

Bibliography

Adler, Kevin F., and Donald W. Burnes. *When We Walk By: Forgotten Humanity, Broken Systems, and the Role We Can Each Play in Ending Homelessness in America.* Berkeley: North Atlantic, 2023.

Allen, Danielle, et al. *Our Common Purpose: Reinventing American Democracy for the 21st Century.* Cambridge: American Academy of Arts and Sciences, 2020.

American Experience. "Have You No Decency?" PBS, Jan. 2, 2020. Video, 5:46. https://www.youtube.com/watch?v=svUyYzzv6VI.

Armstrong, Karen. *Compassion: An Urgent Global Imperative.* Washington, DC: Brookings, 2012.

Associated Press. "War Heroes Are Among 26,000 Images Flagged for Removal in Pentagon's DEI Purge." NPR, Mar. 7, 2025. https://www.npr.org/2025/03/07/nx-s1-5321003/pentagon-images-flagged-removal-dei-purge-trump.

Bailie, Gil. *Violence Unveiled: Humanity at the Crossroads.* New York: Crossroad, 1996.

Bellah, Robert N., et al. *The Good Society.* New York: Random House, 1992.

———. *Habits of the Heart.* New York: Harper & Row, 1985.

Bole, Cliff, dir. "The Best of Both Worlds." *Star Trek: The Next Generation,* season 3, episode 26. Aired June 16, 1990.

Brooks, David. *How to Know a Person: The Art of Seeing Others Deeply and Being Deeply Seen.* New York: Random House, 2023.

———. "What's Happening Is Not Normal. America Needs an Uprising That Is Not Normal." *New York Times,* Apr. 17, 2025.

Bruner, Raisa. "Michelle Obama Explains What 'Going High' Really Means." *Time,* Nov. 20, 2018. https://time.com/tag/michelle-obama/feed/.

Buccola, Nicholas. *The Fire Is Upon Us: James Baldwin, William F. Buckley, Jr., and the Debate over Race in America.* Princeton: Princeton University Press, 2019.

Buechner, Frederick. *Wishful Thinking: A Seeker's ABC.* San Francisco: HarperOne, 1993.

Caldwell, Kristin. "A Blessing for Our People to Come Back Home." Greater NW News, May 5, 2021. https://greaternw.org/news/a-blessing-for-our-people-to-come-back-home/.

Carnegie. Andrew. *The "Gospel of Wealth" Essays and Other Writings*. New York: Penguin, 2006.

Carter, Jimmy. "Crisis of Confidence." The Carter Center, speech delivered July 14, 1979. https://www.cartercenter.org/news/editorials_speeches/crisis_of_confidence.html.

Chodron, Pema. *The Pocket Pema Chodron*. Boston: Shambhala, 2008.

Cleveland Clinic. "Empathy: The Human Connection to Patient Care." YouTube, Feb. 27, 2013. Video, 4:23. https://www.youtube.com/watch?v=cDDWvj_q-o8.

Columbia University Libraries. "Philanthropy of Andrew Carnegie." Rare Book and Manuscript Library. https://library.columbia.edu/libraries/rbml/units/carnegie/andrew.html.

Cooper, William. "Defining the Four Pillars of Trumpism." *Oregonian*, Apr. 15, 2025.

Dalai Lama and Desmond Tutu. *The Book of Joy*. New York: Avery, 2016.

Dans, Paul, and Steven Groves. *Mandate for Leadership 2025: The Conservative Promise*; Project 2025. Washington, DC: Heritage Foundation, 2023.

Davis, Adam. "DOGE Slashed Federal Humanities Funding. Here's How We're Responding." Oregon Humanities, LinkedIn, Apr. 11, 2025. https://www.linkedin.com/pulse/doge-slashed-federal-humanities-funding-heres-how-were-rwj7c/.

De Botton, Alain. *The Art of Travel*. New York: Pantheon, 2002.

Doblmeier, Martin, dir. *Bonhoeffer*. Featuring Klaus Maria Brandauer and Adele Schmidt. New York: First Run, 2003.

Dresner, Samuel. Introduction to *I Asked for Wonder*, by Abraham Heschel. New York: Crossroad, 1993.

Evans, Ben. "Man Who Beat Civil Rights Leader Asks Forgiveness." *San Diego Union-Tribune*, Feb. 5, 2009.

Evans, Russell. "School Violence: Can This Buddhist Practice Make a Difference?" *Lion's Roar*, Jan. 17, 2013. https://www.lionsroar.com/school-violence-can-loving-kindness-make-a-difference/.

Foster, Richard. *Celebration of Discipline: The Path to Spiritual Growth*. New York: Harper Collins, 1978.

Grabenstein, Hannah. "Watch: Trump Says U.S. 'Will Be Woke No Longer.'" PBS News, Mar. 4, 2025. https://www.pbs.org/newshour/politics/watch-trump-says-u-s-will-be-woke-no-longer.

Graham, David A. *The Project: How Project 2025 Is Reshaping America*. New York: Random, 2025.

Greathouse, Lowell. *Rediscovering the Spirit*. Eugene: Wipf & Stock, 2020.

Griffin, Chante. *Loving Your Black Neighbor as Yourself: A Guide to Closing the Space Between Us*. Colorado Springs, CO: WaterBrook, 2024.

Guelzo, Allen C. *The American Mind.* The Great Courses. Chantilly: The Teaching Company, 2005.

Guzman, Mónica. *I Never Thought of It That Way: How to Have Fearlessly Curious Conversations in Dangerously Divided Times.* Dallas: BenBella, 2022.

Haass, Richard. *The Bill of Obligations: The Ten Habits of Good Citizens.* New York: Penguin, 2023.

Hamilton, Alexander, et al. *The Federalist Papers.* New York: New American Library, 1961.

Helliwell, John F., et al., eds. *The World Happiness Report 2025.* Oxford: University of Oxford Wellbeing Research Centre, 2025.

Kabat-Zinn, Jon. *Coming to Our Senses: Healing Ourselves and the World Through Mindfulness.* New York: Hyperion, 2005.

Kabat-Zinn, Jon, and Melvin McLeod. "The Power of Awareness: Jon Kabat-Zinn in Conversation." *Lion's Roar* 10 (2025) 63–67, 76.

Kamenetz, Anya, and Meribah Knight. "Schools Are Embracing Mindfulness, but Practice Doesn't Always Make Perfect." NPR, Feb. 27, 2020. https://www.npr.org/2020/02/27/804971750/schools-are-embracing-mindfulness-but-practice-doesnt-always-make-perfect.

Kennedy, Robert F. *To Seek a Newer World.* New York: Bantam, 1967.

Kiely, Eugene, et al. "A Guide to Project 2025." FactCheck, Sept. 10, 2024. https://www.factcheck.org/2024/09/a-guide-to-project-2025/.

King, Martin Luther, Jr. *Strength to Love.* Philadelphia: Fortress, 1963.

King, Maxwell. *The Good Neighbor: The Life and Work of Fred Rogers.* New York: Abrams, 2018.

Kowitt, Beth. "The Old Model of Billionaire Philanthropy Is Ending." *Oregonian,* May 19, 2025.

Kretzmann, John, and John McKnight. *Building Communities from the Inside Out: A Path Toward Finding and Mobilizing a Community's Assets.* Chicago: ACTA, 1993.

Lakoff, George, and Mark Johnson. *Metaphors We Live By.* Chicago: University of Chicago Press, 1980.

Le Guin, Ursula K. *Lao Tzu: Tao Te Ching; A Book About the Way and the Power of the Way.* Boston: Shambala, 2009.

Leslie, Ian. *Curious: The Desire to Know and Why Your Future Depends on It.* New York: Basic, 2014.

Levine, Barry, and Monique El-Faizy. *All the President's Women: Donald Trump and the Making of a Predator.* New York: Hachette, 2019.

Lewis, John. *Carry On: Reflections for a New Generation.* New York: Grand Central, 2021.

———. *Walking with the Wind.* New York: Simon & Schuster, 1998.

Lewis, Sinclair. *It Can't Happen Here.* New York: Penguin, 1935.

Lieb, David A. "With Trump Targeting DEI, Republican-Led States Intensify Efforts to Stamp It Out." *Oregonian,* May 18, 2025.

Liu, Xianhua, et al. "The Impact of School-Based Mindfulness Intervention on Bullying Behaviors Among Teenagers: Mediating Effect of Self-Control." *Journal of Interpersonal Violence* 37 (2021). https://doi.org/10.1177/08862605211052047.

Lumet, Sidney, dir. *Network*. Los Angeles: United Artists, 1976.

Machado, Antonio. *Fields of Castile/Campos de Castilla: A Dual-Language Book*. Translated by Stanley Appelbaum. Mineola, NY: Dover, 2007.

McCrummen, Stephanie. "Army of God." *Atlantic* 335.2, Feb. 2025, 40–49.

McLaughlin, Corrine, and Gordon Davidson. *Spiritual Politics: Changing the World from the Inside Out*. New York: Ballantine, 1994.

Meacham, Jon. *The Soul of America: The Battle for Our Better Angels*. New York: Random House, 2018.

Moran, Tom. "Trump's Unbound Cruelty, with No Shame." *Oregonian*, Apr. 17, 2025.

Morrison, Toni, ed. *James Baldwin: Collected Essays*. New York: Library of America, 1998.

National Archives. "President John F. Kennedy's Inaugural Address (1961)." Last updated Feb. 8, 2022. https://www.archives.gov/milestone-documents/president-john-f-kennedys-inaugural-address.

Nelson, Greg. "Wallowa Lake Ceremony Honors Return of Land to Nez Perce." Oregon-Idaho Conference, Aug. 2, 2018. https://www.umoi.org/newsdetail/wallowa-lake-ceremony-honors-rightful-return-of-land-to-nez-perce-11627405.

Noah, Timothy. "Fighting Back: A Citizen's Guide to Resistance." *New Republic*, Mar. 27, 2025. https://newrepublic.com/article/193193/fighting-back-citizen-guide-resistance.

Norris, Michele. *Our Hidden Conversations: What Americans Really Think About Race and Identity*. New York: Simon & Schuster, 2024.

NPR. "Read Martin Luther King Jr.'s 'I Have a Dream' Speech in Its Entirety." Last updated Jan. 16, 2023. https://www.npr.org/2010/01/18/122701268/i-have-a-dream-speech-in-its-entirety.

Oregon Humanities. "How Federal Funding Cuts Impact Oregon Humanities." May 19, 2025. https://oregonhumanities.org/who/advocacy/advocacy-FAQ/.

Orwell, George. *Animal Farm*. New York: Penguin, 1996.

Palmer, Parker. *Healing the Heart of Democracy: The Courage to Create a Politics Worthy of the Human Spirit*. San Francisco: Jossey-Bass, 2011.

———. *A Hidden Wholeness: The Journey Toward an Undivided Life*. San Francisco: Jossey-Bass, 2004.

———. *Let Your Life Speak: Listening for the Voice of Vocation*. San Francisco: Jossey-Bass, 2000.

Podplesky, Azaria. "'We Travel in Order to Learn from Culture Shock': Rick Steves Shares Lessons from His Adventures at Northern Quest." *Spokesman-Review*, Apr. 20, 2025. https://www.spokesman.com/stories/2025/apr/20/we-travel-in-order-to-learn-from-culture-shock-ric/.

Purdy, Mike. "An Extraordinary Presidential Statement About an Extraordinary President." Presidential History, Apr. 27, 2015. https://presidentialhistory. com/2015/04/what-did-john-f-kennedy-think-about-thomas-jefferson. html.

Putnam, Robert. *Bowling Alone: The Collapse and Revival of American Community.* New York: Simon & Schuster, 2000.

Putnam, Robert, and Lewis Feldstein. *Better Together: Restoring the American Community.* New York: Simon & Schuster, 2003.

Reagan, Ronald. "The President's News Conference." Ronald Reagan Presidential Library and Museum, conference given on Aug. 12, 1986. https://www. reaganlibrary.gov/archives/speech/presidents-news-conference-23.

Ressa, Maria. *How to Stand Up to a Dictator.* New York: Harper Perennial, 2022.

Rhodes, Ben. *After the Fall: Being American in the World We've Made.* New York: Random House, 2021.

Rogers, Frank, Jr. *Practicing Compassion.* Nashville: Upper Room, 2015.

Rohr, Richard. "Transforming Pain." Center for Action and Contemplation (blog), Oct. 17, 2018. https://cac.org/daily-meditations/transforming-pain-2018-10-17/.

Salles, Walter, dir. *I'm Still Here.* Based on the book by Marcelo Rubens Paiva, screenplay by Murilo Hauser and Heitor Lorega. Culver City, CA: Sony Pictures, 2024.

Southern Poverty Law Center. *Divide, Demoralize, Dismantle: The Hard Right Is Breaking Democracy.* The Year in Hate and Extremism report. Montgomery, AL: Southern Poverty Law Center, 2024.

Synder, Timothy. *On Tyranny.* New York: Crown, 2017.

Terrell, Ellen. "When a Quote Is Not (Exactly) a Quote: The Business of America Is Business Edition." Library of Congress Blogs, Jan. 17, 2019. https:// blogs.loc.gov/inside_adams/2019/01/when-a-quote-is-not-exactly-a-quote-the-business-of-america-is-business-edition/.

Thich Nhat Hanh. *How to Sit.* Berkeley: Parallax, 2014.

———. "Walking Meditation." https://tnhmeditation.org/walking/.

Thompson, Derek. "The Anti-Social Century." *Atlantic* 335.2, Feb. 2025, 26–38.

Thunberg, Greta. *No One Is Too Small to Make a Difference.* New York: Penguin, 2018.

Thurman, Howard. *Jesus and the Disinherited.* Boston: Beacon, 1996.

———. *Meditations of the Heart.* New York: Harper & Brothers, 1953.

———. *The Search for Common Ground.* New York: Harper & Row, 1971.

Trump, Mary L. *Too Much and Never Enough.* New York: Simon & Schuster, 2020.

Turkle, Sherry. *Reclaiming Conversation: The Power to Talk in a Digital Age.* New York: Penguin, 2015.

United States Senate. "Have You No Sense of Decency?" June 9, 1954. https:// www.senate.gov/about/powers-procedures/investigations/mccarthy-hearings/have-you-no-sense-of-decency.htm.

Bibliography

Walsh, Roger. *Essential Spirituality: Exercises from the World's Religions to Cultivate Kindness, Love, Joy, Peace, Vision, Wisdom, and Generosity.* New York: Wiley & Sons, 1999.

Wheatley, Margaret J. *Finding Our Way: Leadership for an Uncertain Time.* San Francisco: Berett-Koehler, 2005.

———. *Turning to One Another: Simple Conversations to Restore Hope in the Future.* San Francisco: Berrett-Koehler, 2002.

Yaconelli, Mark. *Between the Listening and the Telling.* Minneapolis: Broadleaf, 2022.

www.ingramcontent.com/pod-product-compliance
Lightning Source LLC
Chambersburg PA
CBHW072156270326
41930CB00011B/2444